The Limits of Russian Manipulation

National Identity and the Origins of the War in Ukraine

CLINT REACH, RYAN BAUER, ALYSSA DEMUS, KHRYSTYNA HOLYNSKA

Prepared for the U.S. European Command
Approved for public release; distribution is unlimited

NATIONAL DEFENSE RESEARCH INSTITUTE

For more information on this publication, visit **www.rand.org/t/RRA2061-1**.

About RAND

The RAND Corporation is a research organization that develops solutions to public policy challenges to help make communities throughout the world safer and more secure, healthier and more prosperous. RAND is nonprofit, nonpartisan, and committed to the public interest. To learn more about RAND, visit www.rand.org.

Research Integrity

Our mission to help improve policy and decisionmaking through research and analysis is enabled through our core values of quality and objectivity and our unwavering commitment to the highest level of integrity and ethical behavior. To help ensure our research and analysis are rigorous, objective, and nonpartisan, we subject our research publications to a robust and exacting quality-assurance process; avoid both the appearance and reality of financial and other conflicts of interest through staff training, project screening, and a policy of mandatory disclosure; and pursue transparency in our research engagements through our commitment to the open publication of our research findings and recommendations, disclosure of the source of funding of published research, and policies to ensure intellectual independence. For more information, visit www.rand.org/about/principles.

RAND's publications do not necessarily reflect the opinions of its research clients and sponsors.

Published by the RAND Corporation, Santa Monica, Calif.
© 2023 RAND Corporation
RAND® is a registered trademark.

Cover image: The Presidential Office of Ukraine, Sergei Karpukhin/TASS.

About This Report

In this report we discuss Russian manipulation of Ukraine in the post-Soviet period and the origins of the war. In particular, we explore why Russia, which initially had intentions to be a partner in the greater European project, sought to control Ukraine and block any attempt at an independent foreign policy. We also examine why Ukraine, despite close individual ties and shared history and culture with its eastern neighbor, resisted persistent Russian pressure and invasion. The concept we use to interrogate these questions is *national identity*, which became a critical friction point in the Russia-Ukraine confrontation after the collapse of the Soviet Union.

The research reported here was completed in May 2023 and underwent security review with the sponsor and the Defense Office of Prepublication and Security Review before public release.

RAND National Security Research Division

This research was sponsored by the Russia Strategic Initiative, U.S. European Command, and conducted within the International Security and Defense Policy Program of the RAND National Security Research Division (NSRD), which operates the National Defense Research Institute (NDRI), a federally funded research and development center sponsored by the Office of the Secretary of Defense, the Joint Staff, the Unified Combatant Commands, the Navy, the Marine Corps, the defense agencies, and the defense intelligence enterprise.

For more information on the RAND International Security and Defense Policy Program, see www.rand.org/nsrd/isdp or contact the director (contact information is provided on the webpage).

Summary

Background and Purpose of This Report

Russia's manipulation of Ukraine in the post-Soviet period, which culminated in a large-scale invasion in 2022, demonstrated that Russia was willing to resort to all means necessary to secure a regional sphere of influence. Ukrainian resistance to Russia's influence campaign and invasion showed the extent to which Ukraine saw its national interests as best served through independence from Russia and, beginning in 2014, integration into Western institutions.

Events could have taken a different direction. Russia and Ukraine share historical, cultural, religious, and interpersonal ties. Russia in the early 1990s appeared to be on a path toward democratization and constructive relations with its neighbors and the rest of Europe. Many Ukrainians also saw their future as an independent country that was part of a greater Europe in some form. Given the alignment of national interests in the early days of the post–Cold War era, conflict was not inevitable. How did things go so wrong?

The purpose of our research was to investigate the origins of Russia's manipulation and invasion of Ukraine. The study began with the following questions:

- Why did Russia seek to manipulate and control Ukraine beginning in the 1990s and ultimately invade the country?
- Why did Ukraine resist Russia's efforts to influence its domestic and foreign policy?

Approach

Our initial review of Russia-Ukraine relations suggested that post-Soviet national identity formation was a critical factor in Russian manipulation and Ukrainian resistance. To investigate this issue, we used the framework shown in Figure S.1. The framework is derived from literature on Russian and Ukrainian culture and history, as well as scholarship on national iden-

FIGURE S.1

National Identity and the Russia-Ukraine Confrontation

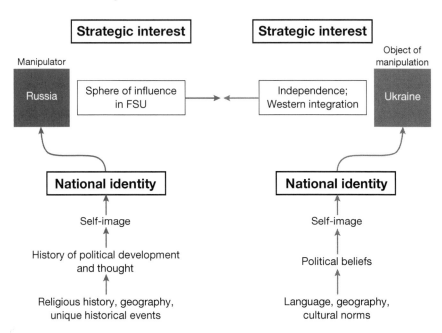

SOURCES: Features information from Shawn T. Thelen and Earl D. Honeycutt, Jr., "National Identity in Russia Between Generations Using the National Identity Scale," *Journal of International Marketing*, Vol. 12, No. 2, 2004; Richard Pipes, *Russian Conservatism and Its Critics: A Study in Political Culture*, Yale University Press, 2007; Rawi Abdelal, Yoshiko M. Herrera, Alastair Iain Johnston, and Rose McDermott, "Identity As a Variable," *Perspectives on Politics*, Vol. 4, No. 4, December 2006; Anne L. Clunan, *The Social Construction of Russia's Resurgence: Aspirations, Identity, and Security Interests*, Johns Hopkins University Press, 2009; Francis Fukuyama, *The Origins of Political Order: From Prehuman Times to the French Revolution*, Farrar, Straus, and Giroux, 2011; Andrei P. Tsygankov, *The Strong State in Russia: Development and Crisis*, Oxford University Press, 2015; Volodymyr Kulyk, "National Identity in Ukraine: Impact of Euromaidan and the War," *Europe-Asia Studies*, Vol. 68, No. 4, April 20, 2016a; Volodymyr Kulyk, "Language and Identity in Ukraine after Euromaidan," *Thesis Eleven*, Vol. 136, No. 1, October 1, 2016b; Joseph Henrich, *The WEIRDest People in the World: How the West Became Psychologically Peculiar and Particularly Prosperous*, Farrar, Straus, and Giroux, 2020.
NOTE: FSU = former Soviet Union.

tity formation. In general, the sources emphasized that religion, language, and geography were important building blocks of the modern political culture and national identity of the two countries. An examination of scholarly works on these subjects led to several findings that help illuminate the underlying causes of Russia's manipulation, Ukrainian resistance, and the war.

Findings

In the early 1990s, there was a brief internal competition for Russia's post-Soviet national identity. There were political camps that wanted Russia to follow a European path of democratization and all of the requisite elements of that process, which might or might not have culminated in formal European integration. But these groups and their vision relatively quickly lost sway within Russia, and more conservative forces took control to return Russia to a more traditional identity as an autocratic, Orthodox, anti-Western great power with imperial aspirations for control beyond the borders of the Russian Federation. The implication of Russia's reversion to historical patterns of autocratic governance and imperial behavior turned out to be existential for Ukraine. Why did Russia follow this path?

Our findings marginalize the idea that external factors such as North Atlantic Treaty Organization (NATO) enlargement was the primary driver of Russian behavior. We note instead that Russia has experienced similar contests for power repeatedly over the past several hundred years. A liberal opposition appears and attempts to dilute central authority, only to be rebuffed by conservative forces who perpetuate the status quo of an autocracy undergirded by the unwavering support of the Orthodox Church. The reason for this outcome is that Russia's religious history has combined with other unique historical events to embed a political culture within Russian society and among the elites that has been impossible for liberal reformers to overturn for any substantial period of time. And this culture helped to form a contemporary national identity among Russians as a distinct and separate entity from Europe, which in turn led Russia to seek a sphere of influence that is incompatible with the post–World War II European regional order and Ukraine's place within it.

Despite some cultural and historical similarities with Russia, post-Soviet Ukraine formed a national identity that was fundamentally at odds with Russia's self-image. This happened for myriad reasons, including the people of Ukraine's distinct development from Russia culturally, historically, and politically. Although Ukraine's post-Soviet national identity formation was far from smooth or uniform across the country, Russia has taken actions since 2014 that unified Ukrainians around an image of their country that is independent of Russia with contrary national aspirations. Despite attention in the West to Russian prowess in manipulation, Russia seems to have significantly misjudged the robustness of Ukrainian national identity that led to a series of self-defeating policies in Ukraine over the past two decades.

Key Takeaway

This report highlights the importance of political culture and national identity in analysis of great powers such as Russia (or China), as well as their immediate neighbors. Exploring the origins of these national characteristics can reveal historical patterns to inform our baseline assumptions about future behavior. It also calls attention to the internal cultural and historical forces that arguably are more influential in determining that behavior than Western policy. Future research on great power behavior should incorporate a broader range of anthropological and sociological literature to improve our understanding of our competitors and the nature of intergroup competition.

Contents

Figures

CHAPTER 1

Introduction

Russia's war on Ukraine is the most consequential moment in 21st century Europe. It upended two decades of relative peace and put to rest any remaining hopes that Russia might join a group of nations united by a shared vision for the continent. The full implications of the war remain to be seen, but already it is clear that Europe will not resemble its former self. Ukraine has been devastated by losses in blood and treasure, and its reconstruction will take decades. Military power will play an increasing role in protecting a European project under threat from a revanchist Russia. Notional walls could be replaced by actual ones to demarcate the boundaries of renewed confrontation. The policies the United States and its allies choose to pursue in response to Russia and to help Ukraine will be of great consequence. Those policies, as well as Western security strategy in Europe in the post–Cold War period, should be informed by an understanding of why the war started. This study is devoted to exploring the origins of the war that came after an intermittent, 30-year Russian campaign to manipulate and control Ukraine.

Background

In the early 1990s, the Russian Federation and Ukraine were at a crossroads. After 70 years of Soviet existence, something new would have to take the place of the hammer and sickle. Looking to the West, most countries in Europe at that time supported a national development model based upon democracy, market economies, and protections of rights that enable the former to flourish. This common goal allowed countries with disparate histories, languages, and traditions (and who were former enemies) to cooperate in pursuit of a shared vision. If Russia and Ukraine followed this path together, then perhaps thorny issues such as post-Soviet borders and nationality could be overcome. Indeed, progressive reformers in Russia in the early 1990s promoted "conspicuously pro-Western policies," such as "political and economic integration of Russia into the West," while "moderate liberals" also favored the "Western model of economic and political development," albeit with greater respect for Russia's unique "geopolitical position and its transitional domestic situation."[1] If Russia and Ukraine each rejected this national model, then collectively they, along with Belarus and other post-Soviet republics, could carve out a separate space to develop in parallel or, perhaps, in competition with the rest of Europe.

If the two chose divergent paths, observers of Russia-Ukraine relations predicted there could be problems because of the aspirations for territorial expansion of various anti-Western camps within Russia in the early 1990s (see Figure 1.1). As Alexei Arbatov, an expert on Russian foreign and defense policy, wrote in 1993, "moderate conservatives" in Russia "cannot reconcile themselves to the demise of the Soviet Union" and view Russia "as an independent great power with its own 'sphere of influence.'" Neo-communists and nationalists in Russia are "devoted to the goal of revival of the Russian empire and Russia's superpower role, not on the premises of communism, but on those of Great-Russian nationalism, a fundamentalist version of Russian Orthodox religion, anti-semitism, and a vigorously anti-Western political crusade. They are prepared to reinstate the Soviet Union by military force, and advocate tough policies towards Ukraine . . . ."[2]

Others shared similar concerns, noting, "the internal peace and stability of Ukraine depends critically on Russian and Ukrainian neighbors not developing sharply defined opposing national identities . . . ."[3] The future of relations between Russia and Ukraine hinged on the formation of their

---

[1] Alexei G. Arbatov, "Russia's Foreign Policy Alternatives," *International Security*, Vol. 18, No. 2, Fall 1993, pp. 9–11.

[2] Arbatov, 1993, pp. 13–14.

[3] Anatol Lieven, *Ukraine and Russia: A Fraternal Rivalry*, United States Institute of Peace, 1999, pp. 144–145.

FIGURE 1.1

Typology of Elite Russian National Identities (Self-Image), 1991–2009

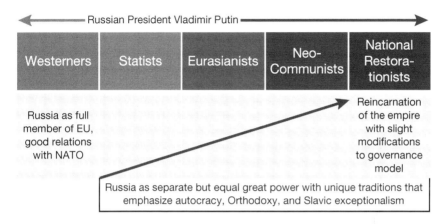

SOURCES: Adapted from Anne L. Clunan, *The Social Construction of Russia's Resurgence: Aspirations, Identity, and Security Interests*, Johns Hopkins University Press, 2009, p. 62. See also Arbatov, 1993, and Vera Tolz, "Forging the Nation: National Identity and Nation Building in Post-Communist Russia," *Europe-Asia Studies*, Vol. 50, No. 6, September 1998.

NOTE: EU = European Union; NATO = North Atlantic Treaty Organization. This figure is slightly adapted from Clunan's 2009 work and presents the leading political identities within Russia throughout the 1990s and the degree of extra-territorial aspirations of each. Putin's place in this political milieu was not obvious when he first came to power in 2000.

post-Soviet national identity, which would either coalesce or compete on the regional end state.[4]

In Russia's case, it was uncertain that Russian elites and a majority of the Russian population would adopt a self-image as a country of the European project based on the aforementioned institutions and values. Russia had little experience with the power-sharing required in a democracy, the Soviet economic system stood in direct contrast to market-based capitalism, and the rights of the individual were not necessarily prioritized above all.[5]

---

[4] Michael E. Urban, "Contending Conceptions of Nation and State in Russian Politics: Defining Ideologies in Post-Soviet Russia," *Demokratizatsiya*, Vol. 1, No. 4, 1992.

[5] Aleksandr Solzhenitsyn, *Rebuilding Russia: Reflections and Tentative Proposals*, Harper Collins Publishers, 1991, pp. 54–78. For the connection between Solzhenitsyn and Putin, see Peter Clement, "Analyzing Russia, Putin, and Ukraine at the CIA and Columbia," *Harriman*, Fall 2022, p. 39.

Nevertheless, experienced foreign policy hands in the United States believed that Russia could successfully transition to democracy and market capitalism, and they linked Russia's potential democratic transition to peace in Europe.

The primary threat at that time to the prospect of Russia embracing an identity as a democratic country with a shared stake in the European project was, according to some, North Atlantic Treaty Organization (NATO) enlargement. As the long-time Russia expert in the State Department, George Kennan, wrote in 1997, expansion of the military alliance had the potential

> to inflame the nationalistic, anti-Western and militaristic tendencies in Russian opinion; to have an adverse effect on the development of Russian democracy; to restore the atmosphere of the cold war to East-West relations, and to impel Russian foreign policy in directions decidedly not to our liking.[6]

Fifty American foreign policy experts signed an open letter to then-President Bill Clinton urging against NATO expansion on similar grounds, negatively correlating NATO's move to the east to Russia's democratic development.[7]

The experts making these arguments were imagining a path for the new Russian Federation that began with external security, which would facilitate Russia's democratic transition and undermine the old guard of Russia who might return and begin to establish a separate sphere of influence over the former Soviet space.[8] It was appropriate to connect Russia's potential democratization to greater peace in Europe. Europe by the early 21st century was as united as any time in modern history. There was a shared vision for the continent based on the tenets discussed above. Were Russia

---

[6] George F. Kennan, "A Fateful Error," *New York Times*, February 5, 1997.

[7] "Opposition to NATO Expansion," Arms Control Association, June 26, 1997.

[8] We should note that many in the U.S. foreign policy establishment—including senior decisionmakers—in the early 1990s did not share the views of Kennan and others and saw NATO enlargement as a stabilizing measure that represented the popular will of the countries involved and that would shore up security in a part of Europe that had been a locus of conflict for centuries.

to pursue similar outcomes, despite the challenges, this could have been a consequential moment for European security and prosperity.[9] Conversely, the argument went, if Russia's external security were to be threatened by NATO enlargement, the nascent democratization process could be irrevocably reversed by undermining Russian reformers and emboldening hard-liners (see Figure 1.2).[10]

One could look at how events transpired over the past three decades and conclude that the origins of Russia's manipulation of Ukraine throughout

FIGURE 1.2

Potential Pathways to Peace or War in Eastern Europe, ~1997

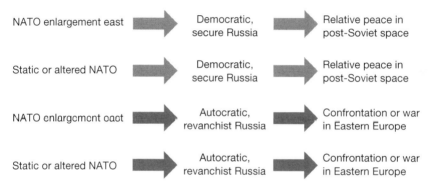

SOURCES: Features information from Kennan, 1997; "Opposition to NATO Expansion," 1997.
NOTE: An autocratic, non-revanchist Russia was less likely because of the need for Russia outside the confines of the European project to establish a separate sphere of influence that would have included Ukraine (Stephen Watts et al., "Alternative Worldviews: Appendixes," RAND Corporation, RR-2982, 2020).

---

[9] To be sure, democracy in Russia could have produced anti-Western outcomes, bringing to power Russian nationalists with territorial aspirations in Ukraine, Kazakhstan, and, perhaps, the Baltic states. See, Neil Malcolm and Alex Pravda, "Democratization and Russian Foreign Policy," *International Affairs*, Vol. 72, No. 3, 1996. At the same time, consolidated democracy would have given more space for moderate and liberal camps to push back against these forces and pursue a more cooperative relationship with the West at a minimum. An additional point to consider is that these nationalist elements in Russia did not believe in democracy as an appropriate political approach for Russia and would not have retained it once in control of the Russian state.

[10] An alternative where NATO did not enlarge, Russia did not pursue a European path built on democracy and market capitalism, and Russia did not meddle in the affairs of its neighbors was probably unlikely for reasons we lay out in Chapter 3 of this report.

the post-Soviet period and subsequent invasions in 2014 and 2022 were largely the result of Western policies that pushed Russia to exactly the place Kennan and others predicted in the mid-1990s.

Such assessments of Russian behavior that emphasize the security aspect have some justification. Policies of the United States and European countries had an impact on the confrontation between Russia and Ukraine. As Putin stated at the outset of Russia's 2022 invasion,

> It is a fact that over the past 30 years we have been patiently trying to come to an agreement with the leading NATO countries regarding the principles of equal and indivisible security in Europe. In response to our proposals, we invariably faced either cynical deception and lies or attempts at pressure and blackmail, while the North Atlantic alliance continued to expand despite our protests and concerns.[11]

Had the West sought a different security architecture after the Cold War, Russia might have come to adopt a less antagonistic model of development and to see itself as a constructive partner in Europe. According to the scholar Michael Mandelbaum, in April 2022, "NATO expansion transformed Russian attitudes from pro-Western to anti-Western, thereby creating the political context that Putin has exploited to conduct his campaigns of aggression."[12] When asked after the war broke out about the wisdom of NATO enlargement, several leading experts on Russia strongly agreed that it was a strategic mistake.[13]

Such arguments are potentially misleading, however, because they create the impression there was an alternative path in which Russia would have embraced a *Euro-centric* identity and thus would not have sought to intervene in the internal affairs of its neighbors against the will of a critical mass (or majority) of citizens of those countries. Because of the history of events, this will forever be an exercise in deliberating a counterfactual. However, future policies and an evaluation of past policies should be informed by a

---

[11] See Max Fisher, "Putin's Case for War, Annotated," *New York Times*, February 24, 2022.

[12] Foreign Affairs, "Was NATO Enlargement a Mistake?" April 19, 2022.

[13] Foreign Affairs, 2022.

comprehensive examination of the circumstances. How one thinks about the future course of the war and a possible end state will be influenced, in part, by a view on why the war started.

Looking at one element of Russia's post-Soviet development—the impact of NATO enlargement—is not sufficient and ignores other important variables within Russia itself. If the idea is that Russia would have acted differently if only the West had pursued different policies is the starting point, then the origins of Russian manipulation and invasion of Ukraine appear to be straightforward. But there are sufficient grounds to question these arguments.

A better lens through which to view the war in Ukraine is the evolution of national identities within Russia and Ukraine from 1991 onward, which were a continuation of the long histories of the people who occupy those lands. As we will show in this report, this is because a consequential portion of Russia's elite and population never embraced the idea that Russia or Ukraine were a part of a European home built upon political and societal norms that are, in general, agreed upon throughout the rest of post–Cold War Europe. It is true that in the early 1990s there was rhetorical support in polling for Russia's democratic path, although the results were far from unanimous.[14] And while there were at first some westernizing forces in Russia, led by figures such as Andrei Kozyrev and Yegor Gaidar, the political tide began turning away from the pro-Western reformers before NATO enlargements in 1999 and 2004.[15] As important, there is a long history in Russia of the victories of the conservative, anti-Western vision over the liberal opposition (see Chapter 3), which again suggests that other factors might have been more influential for Russia's political development and foreign policy toward Ukraine.

By contrast, Ukrainians held views of their country that were fundamentally at odds with the beliefs of many Russian elites and members of society. Ukrainians from the beginning of the post-Soviet period desired an independent state. In December 1991, Ukraine held a nationwide referendum on its independence in which it asked, "Do you support the Declara-

[14] Fredric J. Fleron, Jr., "Post-Soviet Political Culture in Russia: An Assessment of Recent Empirical Investigations," *Europe-Asia Studies*, Vol. 48, No. 2, March 1996.

[15] Urban, 1992, p. 12.

tion of Independence of Ukraine?" followed by a copy of the Declaration's text. As scholar Paul D'Anieri notes,

> the result was overwhelming: 92.3 percent voted in favor of independence. In every single region of Ukraine, *including* Crimea and the city of Sevastopol, a majority supported independence. However, in Crimea and Sevastopol, the majorities were much smaller than elsewhere: 54.2 and 57.1 percent, respectively. In both Donetsk and Luhansk oblasts, 83.9 percent voted for independence.[16]

When searching for the origins of Russian and Ukrainian behavior, we should resist the urge to start with the United States and the collective West as the sun whose forces of gravity affect all other elements within its pull. The point of analytical departure must be Russia and Ukraine themselves, both of whom have been influenced by Western actions but whose behavior is, most of all, a product of internal forces that have been evolving for centuries.

Research Questions and Approach

During our study, we viewed Russian and Ukrainian post-Soviet national identity formation as the critical factor in the origins of the war. In particular, we were interested in the ways in which elites and publics in Russia and Ukraine characterize their national identities which, as Anne Clunan argues, "consist of two pillars: beliefs about a state's appropriate system of governance and mission . . . and ideas about a state's international status . . . ."[17]

Several useful books have already detailed the post-Soviet history of Russo-Ukrainian relations, so we do not spend much time recounting those

---

[16] Paul D'Anieri, *Ukraine and Russia: From Civilized Divorce to Uncivil War*, Cambridge University Press, 2019, p. 34. To be sure, this issue of independence and Ukrainian views on it over time requires a more nuanced discussion, which we present in the latter half of Chapter 4.

[17] Clunan, 2009, p. 10.

facts in Chapter 2.[18] Instead, we highlight the chronology of Russian manipulation of Ukrainian politics and foreign policy in the two decades prior to Russia's first invasion of Ukraine in 2014. This shows that, well before NATO became a plausible threat to Russian interests in Ukraine, Russia was backsliding into an authoritarian form of government and meddling in Ukrainian affairs. Ukrainian elites and a majority of the population meanwhile consistently came down in favor of independence from Russian influence and, in some cases, of a pro-Western orientation.

This leads to the research questions we address in Chapters 3 and 4.

- Why did Russia seek to manipulate and control Ukraine beginning in the 1990s and ultimately invade the country?
- Why did Ukraine resist Russia's persistent efforts to influence its domestic and foreign policy?

To answer these questions, we consulted literature on national identity to build frameworks to guide our examination of this topic.

Based on the diverse expertise and background of the authors of this report, the disparate scholarship on Russia and Ukraine, and the countries' unique internal makeups and paths of development, the chapters on Russian and Ukrainian national identity formation (3 and 4) rely on different literature and take alternative approaches to answer the above questions.[19] The goal of both chapters nevertheless is to provide an explanation for the formation of post-Soviet national identities for Russia and Ukraine. The sections immediately below summarize those different approaches, which are combined into a single framework in Figure 1.3.

---

[18] D'Anieri, 2019; Samuel Charap and Timothy Colton, *Everyone Loses: The Ukraine Crisis and the Ruinous Contest for Post-Soviet Eurasia*, Routledge, 2017; Serhii Plokhy, *Lost Kingdom: The Quest for Empire and the Making of the Russian Nation*, Basic Books, 2017. The last work is a centuries-long historical survey of Russo-Ukrainian relations that includes a discussion of the contemporary dynamics.

[19] The authors of Chapter 4 have expertise in Ukrainian history, politics, and culture and consulted corresponding literature to develop their approach to Ukrainian identity formation. The author of Chapter 3 has a background in Russia studies and used sources that emphasized aspects of Russian national identity formation that were distinct from those found in sources on Ukraine.

FIGURE 1.3

National Identity and the Russia-Ukraine Confrontation

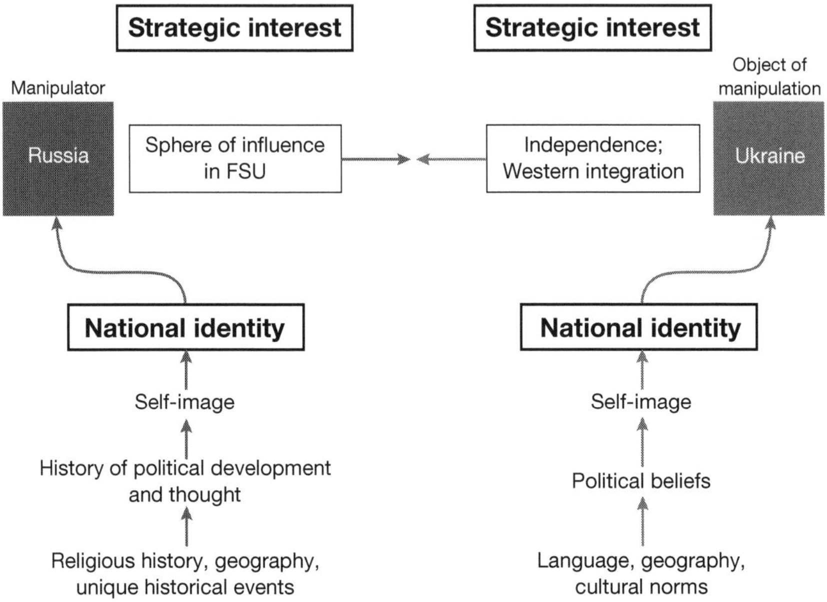

SOURCES: Shawn T. Thelen and Earl D. Honeycutt, Jr., "National Identity in Russia Between Generations Using the National Identity Scale," *Journal of International Marketing*, Vol. 12, No. 2, 2004; Richard Pipes, *Russian Conservatism and Its Critics: A Study in Political Culture*, Yale University Press, 2007; Rawi Abdelal, Yoshiko M. Herrera, Alastair Iain Johnston, and Rose McDermott, "Identity As a Variable," Perspectives on Politics, Vol. 4, No. 4, December 2006; Clunan, 2009; Francis Fukuyama, The Origins of Political Order: From Prehuman Times to the French Revolution, Farrar, Starus, and Giroux, 2011; Andrei P. Tsygankov, *The Strong State in Russia: Development and Crisis*, Oxford University Press, 2015; Volodymyr Kulyk, "National Identity in Ukraine: Impact of Euromaidan and the War," *Europe-Asia Studies*, Vol. 68, No. 4, April 20, 2016a; Volodymyr Kulyk, "Language and Identity in Ukraine after Euromaidan," *Thesis Eleven*, Vol. 136, No. 1, October 1, 2016b; Joseph Henrich, *The WEIRDest People in the World: How the West Became Psychologically Peculiar and Particularly Posperous*, Farrar, Straus, and Giroux, 2020.
NOTE: FSU = former Soviet Union.

Russia

Diverse literature influenced the development of our argument for Russian national identity formation. In her theory of aspirational constructivism, Clunan explained how self-image (identity) among elites and, to a lesser extent, the population lead to collectively held national aspirations.[20] Within Russia, she described a competition for validity of various strains of national self-image from *westernizers*, who saw Russia as a country prepared and best suited to enter the community of European nations, to *national restorationists*, who considered Russia a fundamentally anti-Western country whose purpose lay in building an autocratic state and confronting the collective West to regain Russian influence in its region and great power status (see Figure 1.1 above). Hill and Gaddy also closely detailed the ideological debates within Russia throughout the 1990s and early 2000s and showed how Putin and other conservative forces within Russia continually return to history, language, and Orthodox religion as the foundation of Russia's national identity and role within its region and the world.[21] In a more recent study of *Putinism*, Taylor identified a gradual consolidation around conservatism and anti-Westernism in Russian political culture under Putin.[22]

As Pipes explained in his 2007 study of Russian political culture, versions of the anti-Western identities that Taylor, Clunan, and Hill and Gaddy respectively referred to have prevailed over westernizing forces within Russia over the past three centuries because of the way Russia developed that was distinct from much of the rest of Europe.[23] Tsygankov traces this same pattern in Russia back to the 16th century.[24]

But what about the origins of this culture and its role in determining national identity? The anthropologist Joseph Henrich, in a broad look at national differentiation between the West and much of the rest of the world, argued that religion has played a key role in the psychological, cultural, and

---

[20] Clunan, 2009, p. 62. For an additional article helpful in the initial formulation of this research see David Svarin, "The Construction of 'Geopolitical Spaces' in Russian Foreign Policy Discourse Before and After the Ukraine Crisis," *Journal of Eurasian Studies*, No. 7, 2016.

[21] Fiona Hill and Clifford G. Gaddy, *Mr. Putin: Operative in the Kremlin*, Brookings Institution Press, 2015, pp. 38–62.

[22] Brian Taylor, *The Code of Putinism*, Oxford University Press, 2018. See also Reach, 2020, pp. 21–32; and Watts et al., 2020.

[23] Pipes, 2007.

[24] Tsygankov, 2015, p. 7.

political evolution of countries.[25] Francis Fukuyama covered some similar ground a decade prior in *The Origins of the Political Order*, in which he tried to identify key factors in the divergence of political development across different societies in Europe and Asia.[26] Collectively, this literature helps to guide our research on the continuity of Russian national identity that Putin and senior Russian leaders inherited and perpetuated up to February 24, 2022.

Ukraine

For our analysis of Ukraine, we adapted the conceptions presented by two sets of scholars—Abdelal and colleagues and Shulman—which we amalgamate into our own general framework.[27] Abdelal and colleagues offer a typology for collective identity informed by the existing literature on the subject. Their conception of identity is designed such that it can be used to characterize the collective identity of any group, large or small, from a nation state to a local book club. Shulman, on the other hand, focused more narrowly on national identity, one form of the collective identity characterized by Abdelal and colleagues.[28]

Applying the framework, we examine Ukrainian national identity through three core features and several relevant subfeatures. The first main feature is the *content* of national identity. *Content* refers to the "meaning of a collective identity," or the core essence of what unifies groups and differentiates them from others.[29] The Ukrainian language (and in some subgroups the Russian language), Ukrainian cultural norms and customs,

---

[25] Henrich, 2020.

[26] Fukuyama, 2011, pp. 229–303.

[27] Lastly, before delving into the constituent pieces of Ukrainian national identity, it is important to note that we do not claim that this framework is the most comprehensive or exhaustive. This is not a study intended to adjudicate among competing conceptions of national identity, nor is it a study meant to contribute to the theoretical underpinnings of national identity. Rather, we have chosen to adapt these two approaches as a way to organize our discussion of the core attributes of Ukrainian national identity.

[28] Stephen Shulman, "The Contours of Civic and Ethnic National Identification in Ukraine," *Europe-Asia Studies*, Vol. 56, No. 1, January 1, 2004.

[29] Abdelal et al., 2006, p. 696.

political beliefs, and other features all make up the content of Ukraine's identity. According to Abdelal and colleagues, the content of a group's identity can be described using four subtraits—constitutive norms, social purposes, relational comparisons, and cognitive models.

Contestation, the second feature, refers to the cohesiveness of the group's conception of itself.[30] Prior to Russia's 2014 annexation of Crimea and invasion of the Donbas, tensions over language contributed to fissures in Ukrainian national identity (a higher degree of contestation). Surveys show that since 2014, and particularly since February 24, 2022, many more Ukrainians are learning the Ukrainian language, citing language as a feature of national identity and as a political statement as their rationale.[31] If true, this suggests contestation among those identifying as Ukrainians has waned since 2014, and again since the 2022 invasion.

Lastly, the *intensity* with which members of a group feel unified by their collective traits is another important means by which to characterize a group's national identity. It stands to reason that the intensity of Ukrainian national identity has magnified as the external Russian threats to Ukraine have escalated over the past decade, a trend which we will discuss in detail below.

Scholars have also identified two additional dimensions by which to conceptualize national identity. For some, national identity is thought of in *ethnic* terms, meaning a group's collective cultural traits and shared biological origins agnostic of any territorial boundaries or state structures. For others, it is conceptualized in *civic* terms, meaning it refers to peoples bound via political structures like a state government.[32]

This distinction is important in the context of this chapter given that Ukrainian national identity has evolved along these axes in the post–Cold War era. Before Ukrainian independence in 1991, Ukrainian national identity was overwhelmingly ethnic in nature. After all, a separate Ukrainian

---

[30] Abdelal et al., 2006, p. 696.

[31] Rating Group, "The Sixth National Poll: The Language Issue in Ukraine (March 19, 2022)," webpage, March 25, 2022a; Rating Group, "Seventeenth National Survey: Identity. Patriotism. Values (August 17–18, 2022)," webpage, August 17, 2022b.

[32] Volodymyr Kulyk, "National Identity in Ukraine: Impact of Euromaidan and the War," *Europe-Asia Studies*, Vol. 68, No. 4, April 20, 2016a, pp. 590–592.

state by which to define oneself was nonexistent. But, as political scientist Volodymyr Kulyk writes, "with the establishment of an independent state, Ukrainian identity started gaining in salience and shifting toward civic content, while its ethnocultural basis was gradually acquiring elements that had been suppressed by the Soviet regime as 'nationalistic.'"[33] Even so, the *content* of Ukraine's evolving identity was far from consonant. As we elaborated in the next section, existing cleavages within Ukrainian identity persisted, and were in some cases, deliberately leveraged by elites and politicians in the post-independence era.[34]

Since Russia's annexation of Crimea and its incursions into the Donbas in 2014, however, the scholarship of Kulyk and others has found that Ukrainian identity has undergone a profound change in the form of "increased self-identification as Ukrainian, stronger attachment to symbols of nationhood, enhanced solidarity with compatriots, increased readiness to defend Ukraine or work for Ukraine, and increased confidence in the people's power to change the country for the better."[35] Using the vocabulary of this framework, the strength of Ukrainian national identity has swelled while the degree of contestation on what it means to be a Ukrainian appears to have waned.

---

[33] Kulyk, 2016a, p. 591.

[34] Kulyk, 2016a, p. 591.

[35] Kulyk, 2016a, p. 588; Nadiia Bureiko and Teodor Lucian Moga, "The Ukrainian-Russian Linguistic Dyad and Its Impact on National Identity in Ukraine," *Europe-Asia Studies*, Vol. 71, No. 1, February 2019, p. 142.

CHAPTER 2

Russian Manipulation of Ukraine in the Post-Soviet Period

Though Western actions affected relations between Ukraine and Russia, much of this relationship was shaped by Ukraine's and Russia's contrasting beliefs and objectives. The most enduring challenge that reflects the differences has been Russia's desire to maintain influence over Ukraine, while Ukraine has sought to preserve its independence and sovereignty. In Russia's view, the dissolution of the Soviet Union did not meaningfully change either the role Russia should play in the region or the extensive historical and cultural relations Russia had with its neighbors, particularly Ukraine. Russians have historically viewed Ukrainians as part of the Russian state, which traces its origins and identity to Kyivan (Kievan) Rus'. This notion has been built into the identity of Russia, and the separation of Ukraine meant the loss of Kyiv, which "is tantamount to [Russians] losing a significant part of their cultural and historical identity."[1] Russian elites have struggled to comprehend a Ukrainian state separate from Russia, and many were convinced early on that Ukraine's independence would be temporary.[2] With the need to control Ukraine serving as a key feature of preserving Russia's identity and great-power status, "Russia's notion of its national security was incompatible with Ukraine's democracy and independence."[3]

---

[1] Stephen R. Burant, "Foreign Policy and National Identity: A Comparison of Ukraine and Belarus," *Europe-Asia Studies*, November 1995, Vol. 47, No. 7, November 1995, p. 1137.

[2] Stephen R. Burant, 1995, p. 1137.

[3] D'Anieri, 2019, p. 3.

This underlying belief is demonstrated by various actions Russia has taken since 1991 to further integrate Ukraine and exert Russian interests in violation of Ukraine's territorial and political sovereignty, which this chapter will briefly detail. This chapter will show a pattern of Russia's tactics to shape Ukrainian decisionmaking since the 1990s in an effort "to apply as much pressure across as many fronts as possible" to achieve Russia's desired objectives.[4] These tactics (presented in the text box) include economic measures such as the weaponization of energy; political measures such as direct threats and issuing passports to the citizens of other countries; and promoting separatism and condemning pro-Western figures and policies, as well as broader narratives of Russian's historical and cultural connections with Ukraine.[5] The chapter will primarily focus on the period prior to Russia's invasion in 2014, once it recognized its failure to manipulate Ukrainian decisionmaking and resorted to military measures. We will briefly highlight the continuation of these efforts up to Russia's second invasion of Ukraine in 2022.

1990s: Ukraine Achieves Independence

Dissolution of Soviet Union and Ukraine's Desire for Independence

In 1991, as Ukraine was in the process of negotiating the terms and degree of separation from the Soviet Union, Ukraine held its first direct presidential election and a referendum vote on the country's independence. As evidence of Ukraine's desire for independence, all six of Ukraine's candidates supported independence, and 92 percent of Ukrainians supported the referendum, with every region voting in favor including Crimea and eastern Ukraine (see Figure 2.1).[6] During this time there were some signs that Ukraine might join a revised Union Treaty that both Boris Yeltsin and

---

[4] Ihor Hurak and Paul D'Anieri, "The Evolution of Russian Political Tactics in Ukraine," *Problems of Post-Communism*, Vol. 69, No. 2, 2022, p. 129.

[5] Hurak and D'Anieri, 2022, p. 129.

[6] D'Anieri, 2019, pp. 33–34.

Examples of Russian Manipulation Tactics Against Ukraine

- Political
  - issuing/providing passports
  - promoting separatism
  - legislation that rejected Ukraine's sovereignty
  - integration proposals to Russian-led institutions
  - organization or encouragement of protests
  - withdrawing from treaties, alliances, or trade agreements
  - supporting political candidates or parties
  - infiltrating government organizations and positions of power
- Economic
  - gas cutoffs
  - gas subsidies
  - debt relief
  - financial support to groups to further entrench ethnic and social cleavages
  - financial support to political figures
  - imposing/removing embargoes, duties, tariffs, or sanctions
  - increasing market access control
  - loans and financial support to government
- Information
  - planting, distributing, or promoting fabricated or misleading news
  - promoting revisions history or contentious historical narratives
  - denial including flooding the information space to muddy the facts around an event
  - disparaging pro-Western policies and officials
  - veiled threats by government officials and spokespeople
- Militaristic
  - military harassment
  - supporting proxy forces with military personnel and supplies
  - claiming, annexing, or creating territory (e.g., island-building)
  - purported assassination attempts
  - providing military cover to secession
- Cultural
  - emphasizing cultural and historical connections with Russia
  - using Russian Orthodox Church to intervene in political issues

SOURCE: Features information from Christopher Paul, Michael Schwille, Michael Vasseur, Elizabeth M. Bartels, and Ryan Bauer, *The Role of Information in U.S. Concepts for Strategic Competition*, RAND Corporation, RR-A1256-1, 2022.

NOTE: This is not an exhaustive list of the tactics Russia has employed against Ukraine.

Mikhail Gorbachev sought to develop. The treaty would have assured Russia's formal linkages with Ukraine and other former Soviet states in the form of a single economic market, a shared currency, and a common military structure, controlled by Moscow.[7]

---

[7] D'Anieri, 2019, pp. 34–35.

FIGURE 2.1

1991 Ukrainian Independence Referendum by Region

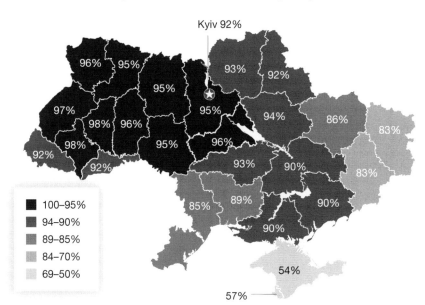

SOURCE: Redrawn from Thomas Young, "10 Maps That Explain Ukraine's Struggle for Independence," *Brookings*, May 21, 2015.

When it came time to finalize the details of the Soviet Union's dissolution, Ukraine's newly elected president Leonid Kravchuk rejected the formation of the Union Treaty. Having recently been empowered by both the presidential election and Ukraine's overwhelming support for independence, Kravchuk wanted Ukraine to be a separate state that was not controlled by Russia.[8] Yeltsin, who was seeking to disband the Soviet Union and sideline Gorbachev, acquiesced to Kravchuk to gain Ukraine's support and disbanded the "Soviet Union without a new union to replace it."[9] To help resolve this disagreement, the Commonwealth of Independent States (CIS) was developed, which Russia sought to operate as a confederation. Ukraine, however, ensured there were no legally binding commitments and never rat-

---

[8] D'Anieri, 2019, p. 34.

[9] D'Anieri, 2019, pp. 33–35.

ified the treaty to become an official member, fearing that Russia would use the organization "as a potential vehicle for Russia's hegemony."[10]

Russia's Desire to Maintain Influence

These diverging objectives help to demonstrate an enduring issue that has plagued Ukrainian-Russian relations since the initial years of Ukraine's independence. Russian authorities seeking to maintain control over the region and Ukraine's opposition to Russian integration efforts. Even Yeltsin, who, by comparison with other Russian leaders, was far more Western-oriented, "sought central control over the republics, especially Ukraine."[11] Moscow's ambassador to the United States, Vladimir Lukin, who was considered more liberal on Russia's political spectrum, stated that "relations between Russia and Ukraine were to be 'identical to those between New York and New Jersey.'"[12] By contrast, Kravchuk, who won the election against a nationalist and received strong support in eastern Ukraine and Crimea, sought to preserve Ukraine's sovereignty.[13]

In the aftermath of the Soviet Union's dissolution, Russia sought to preserve its control over the region through Russian-led projects like the CIS, which was meant to serve as a forcing function to maintain linkages and influence over its neighbor's policies. In the early 1990s, Yeltsin and other Russian authorities spoke about the necessity for integration between Russia and CIS countries and for the international community to respect this. In a 1994 presidential decree, for example, Yeltsin indicated how Russia's vital security and economic interests are concentrated in CIS states and Russia's leading role in developing a new system of relations in the post-Soviet space.[14]

---

[10] Rilka Dragneva and Kataryna Wolczuk, *Ukraine Between the EU and Russia: The Integration Challenge*, Palgrave Macmillan, 2015, p. 15.

[11] Paul D'Anieri, 2019, p. 35.

[12] Charap and Colton, 2017, p. 56.

[13] D'Anieri, 2019, p. 35.

[14] Charap and Colton, 2017, p. 55.

Russia's desire for integration was especially prominent with Ukraine. The Kremlin believed any efforts from Ukraine to rebuff this was the result of Western interference rather than Ukraine pursuing its own interests. Russia's perception, which assumed that Ukraine would not freely choose anything but a Russia-centric orientation, speaks to the lingering issue of how Russians intrinsically view Ukraine as part of Russia. This Russian sense of connection is rooted in the extensive historical and cultural ties between the two countries and is used as a mechanism for Russia to continue to maintain its influence over Ukraine. According to Anatoly Z. Moskalenko, a prominent Ukrainian historian and journalist, "Russians love to refer to the relations between Russia and Ukraine as the relations of an older brother and a younger brother. But in reality, the relationship was like that of a horse and a rider. The rider—Russia—always did everything to prevent the horse—Ukraine—from getting free."[15]

Russia pursued a range of measures to manipulate and control Ukraine in the first decade of Ukraine's independence. One example is Russia providing subsidized energy and natural resources as means to exert influence and receive political and economic concessions. According to one estimate, "Russia has been subsidizing the Ukrainian economy by 5 to 10 billion USD annually since 1991."[16] Russia also sought to use economic coercion to force Ukrainian integration. In the mid-1990s, Russian leaders imposed "excise duties on oil and gas imports" in an effort to strong-arm Ukraine into joining the Russian-led Customs Union.[17] Though Ukraine was interested in economic cooperation with the CIS, Kyiv rejected Russia's tactics because of concern over the political ramifications "and low credibility" of the organization.[18]

---

[15] As cited in Elizabeth Shogren, "In the Shadow of 'Big Brother': Ukraine: Long Under Russia's Thumb, the Newly Independent State Struggles to Change Its Relationship to One of Equals," *Los Angeles Times*, May 1, 1992.

[16] Andrej Krickovic and Maxim Bratersky, "Benevolent Hegemon, Neighborhood Bully, or Regional Security Provider? Russia's Efforts to Promote Regional Integration After the 2013–2014 Ukraine Crisis," *Eurasian Geography and Economics*, Vol. 57, No. 2, 2016, p. 183.

[17] Dragneva and Wolczuk, 2015, p. 17.

[18] Dragneva and Wolczuk, 2015, p. 17.

Of particular interest to Russia was maintaining ownership and control over the Black Sea Fleet. One measure Russia employed was to use Ukraine's gas debt as a means to extract ownership over the fleet and its base in Sevastopol, Crimea.[19] In addition to economic measures, Russia sought to exert pressure on Ukraine's leadership through intimidation, direct territorial threats, and legislative resolutions to maintain its ownership of the Black Sea Fleet and force Ukraine's political integration. For example, in the early 1990s, Russia used various types of intimidation and threats to assert its influence in the area. These included sending ships to hassle a Ukrainian patrol ship in the area, issuing Russian passports to Ukrainians working at Black Sea facilities, and harassing Ukrainian servicemen and stations to the point that it became dangerous "to walk around Sevastopol."[20] Russia media also promoted a disinformation campaign in 1994 that claimed Ukrainian National Guard Natsyks (or Nazis) were preparing to storm Russian Black Army headquarters.[21] Reminiscent of a modern Russian disinformation campaign, the messaging created panic in Sevastopol and led some to beg the Ukrainian Guardsmen "not to kill at least the children."[22]

Russia regularly threatened Ukraine's territorial integrity as a method of forcing Ukraine's participation in regional institutions such as the CIS. For example, Russia claimed that the previous 1990 agreement that promised respect for Ukraine's sovereignty was no longer valid because it was made when both states were part of third state—the Soviet Union.[23] Throughout the 1990s, Russia's legislature also signaled its lack of respect for Ukraine's sovereignty through resolutions calling to reject the legality of Crimea's 1954 transfer to Ukraine and declare ownership over Sevastopol, though Yeltsin vetoed these measures.[24] In a 1992 visit to Crimea by the then–vice president

---

[19] D'Anieri, 2019, p. 41.

[20] Yaroslav Mezentsev, "Cold War for Crimea. How the Fleet Was Divided in the 1990s," *Istoreechna Pravda*, May 10, 2011.

[21] Mezentsev, 2011.

[22] Mezentsev, 2011.

[23] D'Anieri, 2019, p. 54.

[24] D'Anieri, 2019, pp. 44–51; "Yeltsin Assails Parliament Vote Claiming Crimean Port for Russia," *New York Times*, July 11, 1993.

of Russia, Alexander V. Rutskoi, Rutskoi called for the peninsula's seces-sion.[25] An attempt to resolve this issue was the 1997 Russia-Ukraine Friend-ship Treaty, which divided the Black Sea Fleet, settled Ukraine's debt, and, most importantly, "reaffirm[ed] the inviolability of the borders" between Russia and Ukraine.[26] As part of the treaty, Ukraine also acquiesced to join-ing the CIS Inter-Parliamentary Assembly, which had minimal influence but had been a move Ukraine previously opposed.[27] Russia also tried unsuc-cessfully to add language in the treaty "that would have allowed citizens of Ukraine to obtain dual Russian citizenship," in an effort to increase Russia's influence in the country.[28]

Ukraine's Push Toward the West

Despite Russia's efforts, Ukraine continued to defend its national sover-eignty and reject efforts by Russia to integrate Kyiv into Russian-led insti-tutions. Even in 1994, with the election of Ukraine's new president Leonid Kuchma, who was seen as a more pro-Russian figure that advocated for improving economic ties with Russia, Kuchma sought to maintain relations with Russia while also seeking to preserve Ukraine's national identity.[29] Ukraine maintained only an observer status with the CIS and sought to derail Russian initiatives, rejected an invitation to join the Customs Union, and, in 2000, again maintained only an observer status in the Russian-led Eurasian Economic Community (EEC).[30]

Meanwhile, Ukraine signed several agreements with the West in the 1990s (such as the Partnership and Cooperation Agreement with the EU and the Partnership for Peace document with NATO) and was the first CIS country to do so. These actions helped to underscore Ukraine's inter-

---

[25] Richard Boudreaux, "Regional Outlook: Crimea's President a Prisoner of His Own Separatist Revolt: Russia Has Lost Interest in Supporting Yuri Meshkov and His Would-Be Ministate," *Los Angeles Times*, May 23, 1995.

[26] D'Anieri, 2019, p. 82.

[27] Dragneva and Wolczuk, 2015, p. 19.

[28] Burant, 1995, p. 1139.

[29] Burant, 1995, p. 1138.

[30] Charap and Colton, 2017, p. 61; Krickovic and Bratersky, 2016, p. 183.

est to improve relations with Western entities and reject Russian efforts to integrate Ukraine.[31] Ukraine's actions also highlighted a growing concern among Ukrainian policymakers over how NATO's eastward expansion could pigeonhole the country. The growing sense was that expansion might, at best, force Ukraine to serve as "a buffer zone between Russia and an expanded NATO and at worst force it to join the CIS collective security pact."[32] President Kuchma made this sentiment clear during remarks in 2001, when he indicated that "We would not like Ukraine to be a bridge between Europe and Russia—I personally do not like this idea because bridges get trampled upon."[33]

In addition to shifts toward the West, Ukraine also sought to develop its own framework with other former Soviet states. In early 1993, Ukrainian President Kravchuk unsuccessfully proposed a policy of a zone of stability and security with several former Warsaw Pact countries to maintain security in the region in response to a perceived Russian threat.[34] In 1997, abstainers or dropouts from both the Collective Security Treaty Organization (CSTO) and a CIS economic structure formed a group called GUAM (Georgia, Ukraine, Armenia, and Moldova) that struggled to produce specific initiatives but discussed efforts to improve relations with the West.[35] Despite these efforts over the decade, a poll in 2000 showed that Ukrainians continued to have a more positive "view of Russia than of the U.S. or NATO."[36]

During this first decade Ukraine largely sought to reject Russian integration efforts and reduce its interdependence but did not make a fundamental break from Russia given the interconnectivity between the two nations. This is a result of not only historical and cultural ties but also Ukraine's close economic and energy connections to Russia. Russia managed to exploit this reliance, which Ukraine made little progress to reduce, in part because of

---

[31] Burant, 1995, p. 1130.

[32] Burant, 1995, p. 1130.

[33] D'Anieri, 2019, p. 109.

[34] Burant, 1995, p. 1130.

[35] Charap and Colton, 2017, p. 62.

[36] Charap and Colton, 2017, p. 66.

"the rent-seeking strategies of oligarchic interests and the lack of comprehensive economic reform."[37] Ukrainian oligarchs had sought to maintain relations with both the West and Russia to maximize their wealth.[38] While Ukrainian leaders sought the benefits of further integrating with Western institutions, little progress had been made on domestic political and economic reforms.[39]

2000s: Russia's Increasingly Aggressive Manipulation

As Ukraine continued its pursuit of independence, the Kremlin increased its efforts to assert control of Kyiv through a combination of enticements and threats tailored to Kyiv's vulnerabilities and priorities.[40] This is displayed in several events that occurred in the early 2000s, including continued integration proposals, efforts to influence elections, direct threats to Ukrainian sovereignty, the weaponization of gas exports, and fomenting separatism.

Economic Integration Proposals

Russia sought to encourage Ukraine's integration into Putin's first regional integration initiative, the EEC, which, like many projects, saw Ukraine's participation as critical.[41] In pursuit of this objective, Russia pursued several tactics. These included increased rapprochement during a period of waning relations between Ukraine and the West; offering economic incentives, including "exemptions from free trade, antidumping" and lower gas prices; and systematic efforts to promote the economic benefits to Ukrainians and present arguments against EU integration.[42] As noted previously,

---

[37] Dragneva and Wolczuk, 2015, p. 9.

[38] D'Anieri, 2019, p. 74.

[39] D'Anieri, 2019, pp. 95–96.

[40] Dragneva and Wolczuk, 2015, p. 20.

[41] Dragneva and Wolczuk, 2015, p. 20.

[42] Dragneva and Wolczuk, 2015, pp. 20–21.

these efforts resulted only in Ukraine's adoption as an observer of the EEC, leading Russia to propose the Common Economic Space (CES) as an alternative structure. Mindful of the increasing relationship between Ukraine and the EU, the agreement again offered important economic incentives to Ukraine, although there were concerns over the increased authority it would provide to Russia.[43]

2003 Tuzla Island Dispute

One incident that served as foreshadowing of Russia's annexation of Crimea is the 2003 Tuzla Island dispute. In 2003, during discussions of the CES treaty, Russia, without notice, began to build a dam from Russian territory (Taman Peninsula) to Tuzla Island, which was considered part of Crimea. Ukraine argued Russia's actions were an effort to annex the island and gain control over the Kerch Strait. The dispute created heightened tensions between the two countries and concerns that the disagreement would break out into a military conflict, with Putin's chief of staff saying that Russia "will drop bombs" in the strait to maintain its hold and prevent Ukraine from sending troops to protect the island.[44] Russian officials such as Krasnodar Governor Aleksandr Tkachev also proclaimed that Tuzla was historically part of Russia, fueling concerns about Russian encroachment of Ukrainian territory backed by the threat of military use.[45] The incident, however, produced the opposite effect on Ukrainians from what Russia had hoped for. Ukrainians overwhelmingly supported the sending of troops to defend its sovereignty, and President Kuchma warned that "the closer the dam gets to Ukraine, the closer Ukraine gets to the West."[46]

The dispute was settled in a 2003 treaty in which Russia stopped construction of the dam and Ukraine maintained sovereignty and management

---

[43] Dragneva and Wolczuk, 2015, p. 23.

[44] Sophie Lambroschini, "Russia/Ukraine: Prime Ministers Meet Today over Tuzla Dam Dispute," *Radio Free Europe/Radio Liberty*, October 24, 2003.

[45] Lambroschini, 2003.

[46] Kim Murphy, "Russia-Ukraine Ties Founder on the Shore of Tiny Isle," *Los Angeles Times*, November 3, 2003; William Varettoni, "Crimea's Overlooked Instability," *Washington Quarterly*, Vol. 34, No. 3, 2011.

of the channel but at several costs. The treaty ensured that Ukraine would join the CES. The agreement also did not establish clear maritime borders for the Sea of Azov, which Russia had exploited to increase its presence in the area, including through military exercises and stopping and searching vessels that enter the sea.[47] Russia has continued to use the unresolved maritime borders in providing arbitrary interpretations of the legal statuses of the Azov Sea and Kerch Strait to defend its post-2014 actions.[48] Some Ukrainian analysts also suggested that Russia's actions might have been an effort to create a territorial dispute for Ukraine to inhibit its ability to join NATO.[49]

2004 Election and Orange Revolution

During Ukraine's 2004 election, Russia played a direct role in supporting the campaign of its preferred candidate, Viktor Yanukovych. In the lead-up to the election, Putin made well-publicized visits to Ukraine to convey support for Yanukovych. The Kremlin also helped to finance Yanukovych's campaign, including "paying for pro-Yanukovych polling and electoral activities."[50] According to one assessment, the Kremlin reportedly financed nearly half of Yanukovych's campaign expenses, which included two teams of advisors to help manage the Yanukovych campaign.[51]

Another method by which Russia sought to influence the election was through Russian media. For instance, Russian media "praised Yanukovych widely" as the pragmatic choice and "ran negative stories on Yushchenko" who was framed as a puppet of the West.[52] Russian media also sought to convey the importance of maintaining unity between Russia and Ukraine,

---

[47] Vladimir Socor, "Azov Sea, Kerch Strait: Evolution of Their Purported Legal Status (Part Two)," *Jamestown Foundation*, December 5, 2018.

[48] Socor, 2018.

[49] Murphy, 2003.

[50] Charap and Colton, 2017, p. 71.

[51] Derek Fraser, "Taking Ukraine Seriously: Western and Russian Responses to the Orange Revolution," in Oliver Schmidtke and Serhy Yekelchyk, eds., *Europe's Last Frontier?* Palgrave Macmillan, 2008, p. 11; D'Anieri, 2019, p. 129.

[52] D'Anieri, 2019, p. 129.

emphasizing the common history and culture and portraying Yushchenko as seeking to disrupt this bond. Russian figures such as Russia's ambassador to Ukraine, Viktor Chernomyrdin, also highlighted the importance of relations between the two countries, noting that "Ukraine and Russia have never lived as two sovereign states."[53] Russia is also accused of enacting other malign measures to shape the election, including allegations that Moscow was involved in at least two of the assassination attempts against Viktor Yushchenko during the 2004 election.[54]

The 2004 election initially resulted in a publicly disputed second-round vote that had reportedly given Yanukovych the presidency, sparking mass protests within Ukraine known as the Orange Revolution. Russia's actions and perceptions of events during the election and the subsequent protests help to demonstrate Russia's misperception of Ukraine. For example, on the eve of the election, Putin traveled to Kyiv in an effort to sway Ukrainians to vote for the Russia-backed candidate Yanukovych, which, in turn, spurred indignation among Ukrainians that their country's "independence was under threat."[55] In the immediate aftermath of the disputed second-round vote, Putin made "a premature congratulatory call" to Yanukovych.[56] And regarding the protests, Russia perceived this was the result of Western interference rather than Ukrainian opposition to the illegitimate second round of voting.[57] Not only did Ukrainian citizens conduct mass protests in the streets, but Ukrainian oligarchs also played a role in shaping the aftermath of the election, likely fearing a threat to their autonomy from greater Russian control.[58] Support from Ukrainian oligarchs included providing positive news about the protests, maintaining transportation to Kyiv (which had been shut down in previous protests against President Kuchma), and fig-

---

[53] Fraser, 2008, p. 9.

[54] Fraser, 2008, p. 11.

[55] Peter Dickinson, "How Ukraine's Orange Revolution Shaped Twenty-First Century Geopolitics," *Atlantic Council*, November 22, 2020.

[56] Charap and Colton, 2017, p. 71.

[57] D'Anieri, 2019, pp. 131–132.

[58] D'Anieri, 2019, pp. 130–131.

ures such as Kyiv's Mayor Omelchenko denouncing the election results.[59] Overall, the Orange Revolution both shocked and worried the Kremlin about Ukraine's path toward the West and Russia's declining influence over Ukraine.

2005 and 2009 Gas Wars

In both 2005 and 2009, Russia again sought to use energy as a means to increase its control over Ukraine. In 2005, Russia sought to increase its control over the pipeline structure by which Russian gas traveled through Ukraine to reach Europe and increase the price that Ukraine paid for gas. Russia threatened to cancel subsidized gas prices to Ukraine if Kyiv did not agree "to a consortium arrangement for its pipeline network" and briefly interrupted its gas supply to Ukraine before coming to agreement.[60]

Similarly, in 2009, a gas dispute emerged because of an inability to reach an agreement on the price Ukraine would pay for Russian gas and the cost of transiting gas to Europe.[61] During the negotiations process, Russia unexpectedly shut off its gas to Ukraine, demonstrating Russia's frustration with the process and intention to destabilize Ukraine and its economy.[62] The new agreement between Ukraine and Russia was again unfavorable to Ukraine for several reasons, including having to pay higher prices than other countries.[63] These events serve as a clear "demonstration of Moscow's quickness to resort to" coercive economic diplomacy when it perceives a country in its near abroad as going against its wishes.[64] While these efforts might achieve initial objectives, they come at a long-term cost of diminishing trust, a factor that "Russian policy toward the region has rarely taken into

---

[59] D'Anieri, 2019, p. 130.

[60] Charap and Colton, 2017, p. 80.

[61] Jonathan Stern, Simon Pirani, and Katja Yafimava, "The Russo-Ukrainian Gas Dispute of January 2009: A Comprehensive Assessment," Oxford Institute for Energy Studies, February 2009, p. 4.

[62] Lilia Shevtsova, *Lonely Power: Why Russia Has Failed to Become the West and the West Is Weary of Russia*, Carnegie Endowment for International Peace, 2010, p. 160.

[63] D'Anieri, 2019, p. 160.

[64] Charap and Colton, 2017, pp. 80–81.

account."[65] Russia's actions came at a cost of "threatening the reliability of Russian gas transit to Europe."[66] This pattern is reflected again in the current Russia-Ukraine war, with Russia cutting off gas supplies to Europe and possibly even sabotaging Russia's pipeline to Europe.

Russia Fueling Separatism

One measure Russia has used to put pressure on Kyiv to maintain linkages with Russia and inhibit further integration with the West is fomenting separatism in Crimea. In November 2004, during protests after the corrupt second-round election for the Ukrainian presidency, delegates from eastern Ukraine and Crimea came together and "voted to hold a referendum on regional autonomy (federalism, not secession) if Yanukovych were not confirmed as the president."[67] The individuals stood under a Russian Flag and were joined by the mayor of Moscow, who referred to those that opposed the referendum as a "sabbath of witches," though the initiative did not receive enough support from either elites or the public.[68]

In 2006, Ukrainian President Yushchenko grew concerned about Russian intelligence services having a role in promoting separatism in Ukraine and called on the Security Service of Ukraine (SBU) to investigate this. The agency identified links between Russia's intelligence services and subversion in Crimea. In particular, Russian intelligence services were working to assert influence over "the *socio-political* situation in Crimea and the city of Sevastopol" through various means, including spreading propaganda and "creating a position of influence within the regional organs of the government, administration, socio-political spheres and in the mass media sector."[69]

---

[65] Charap and Colton, 2017, pp. 80–81.

[66] Shevtsova, 2010, p. 160.

[67] D'Anieri, 2019, p. 133.

[68] D'Anieri, 2019, p. 133.

[69] Lada L. Roslycky, "Russia's Smart Power in Crimea: Sowing the Seeds of Trust," *Southeast European and Black Sea Studies*, Vol. 11, No. 3, September 2011, p. 303.

Russia also endeavored to promote pro-Russian sentiment in Crimea through other means. For example, pro-Russian non-governmental organizations (NGOs) operating in Crimea were alleged to be supporting separatism in the region with the financial support of the Kremlin, which one expert characterized as Russia's response to the purported role of American-funded NGOs in supporting the Orange Revolution.[70] These organizations conducted various activities in an effort to undermine Ukrainian leadership and unity, from equating NATO and Ukrainian figures to Nazis to publicly calling for Russia to annex Crimea and encouraging Ukrainians to pursue dual citizenship with Russia.[71]

Ukraine's Continued Movement West and the Perceived Threat from Russia

Under President Yushchenko, Ukraine continued its efforts to integrate further toward the West, including NATO's 2008 Bucharest Meeting Memorandum and the EU's 2009 EU Eastern Partnership program. Russia saw NATO's actions as a direct threat to Russia's security and viewed the EU's program to expand eastward as an attempt to increase its influence in the region while disregarding Russia's interests. Russia's State Duma, in fact, proposed a measure to repeal the 1997 Friendship Treaty that confirmed Ukraine's territorial integrity if NATO offered Ukraine a clear plan to join. Putin also expressed that Russia does not consider its neighbors "to be real countries entitled to their own policies," referring to Ukraine as "an artificial creation of capricious Soviet leaders."[72] In August 2008, then–President Dmitry Medvedev asserted Russia's sphere of privileged interest in the region through several principles, including "protecting the lives and dignity of our citizens, wherever they may be."[73] In parallel to this, "the Duma

---

[70] Roslycky, 2011, p. 305.

[71] Roslycky, 2011, p. 307.

[72] Charap and Colton, 2017, p. 89.

[73] D'Anieri, 2019, p. 169.

amended legislation in August 2009 to permit Russian forces to intervene abroad in defense of Russian citizens."[74]

2010–2022: Russia's 2014 and 2022 Invasions

Russia's Actions Leading Up to 2014 Invasion

In 2010, Viktor Yanukovych was elected the next president of Ukraine. He was seen as a more pro-Russian figure than his predecessors and sought to maintain relations with both the West and Russia to achieve the maximum benefits from these relationships. Yanukovych's path toward improved relations with Russia was also likely due in part to Russia's success in embedding Russian personnel into several key positions within Yanukovych's administration. Examples of this include Valeriy Khoroshkovskyy, who served as the SBU Chairman and had "major business interests in Russia and strong ties to the Federal Security Service (FSB)," and the head of the Presidential Guard, Viacheslav Zanevskyi, who was actually a Russian citizen.[75]

Shortly after taking office, Yanukovych signed a "the Kharkiv Pact," which disavowed Ukrainian NATO membership and extended Russia's lease of Crimean naval facilities for its Black Sea Fleet.[76] The Pact, however, did not resolve gas relations between the countries. Shortly after the agreement, Russia again proposed a deal to increase Russia's "control over Ukraine's gas production, transmission systems, internal gas trade and export, as well as nuclear power generation."[77]

Another critical effort was to thwart the progress that Ukraine and the EU had made on their Association Agreement and to encourage Ukraine's participation in the Russian-led Customs Union. Russia offered economic incentives for joining the Customs Union and repeatedly cited harms Ukraine would endure from the EU agreement, including economic (wors-

---

[74] Stephen F. Larrabee, "Russia, Ukraine, and Central Europe: The Return of Geopolitics," *Journal of International Affairs*, Vol. 63, No. 2, 2010.

[75] Taras Kuzio, "Ukraine: Coming to Terms with the Soviet Legacy," *Journal of Communist Studies and Transition Politics*, Vol. 14, No. 4, December 2012, pp. 576–578.

[76] Charap and Colton, 2017, p. 106.

[77] Dragneva and Wolczuk, 2015, p. 65.

ening trade balance with the EU and negative impacts on Ukraine's big businesses) and political (loss of sovereignty in aligning to EU rules without any say in them) losses.[78] Russia also sought to use its cultural appeal and connections to pro-Russian media, for example, "NGOs and civil society groups in Ukraine that would support Russia's interests, particularly in Crimea and the eastern portion of the country."[79] One example of this is the use of the Russian Orthodox Church, which, prior to 2018, "had total jurisdiction over the canonical territory in Ukraine, with almost as many parishes in Ukraine as in Russia."[80]

In addition, Russia pursued harsh economic measures and threats against Ukraine to prevent it from furthering progress on the EU Association Agreement. These included imposing trade sanctions, threatening Ukraine's CIS trade preferences, and direct threats against Ukraine's sovereignty. In particular, Putin advisor Sergei Glazyev stated that, while "[w]e don't want to use any kind of blackmail," if Ukraine signed the EU's Association Agreement, it would violate the Russia-Ukraine 1997 treaty that established Ukraine's borders.[81] As such, "Russia would no longer guarantee Ukraine's statehood and might intervene if pro-Russian regions sought help from Russia."[82] These threats were both consistent with Russia's history of tactics against Ukraine and a foreshadowing of Russia's soon invasion of Ukraine and annexation of Crimea.

Eventually, in November 2013, largely because of pressures and an economic offer from Russia, Yanukovych officially suspended the EU's Association Agreement. In return for the move, "Russia promised to purchase US$15bn in Ukrainian Eurobonds and to cut the gas price for Ukraine" by roughly one-third.[83] In response to the protests that erupted in Ukraine, the Kremlin encouraged Kyiv to forcibly end protests and threatened to with-

---

[78] Dragneva and Wolczuk, 2015, p. 69.

[79] Krickovic and Bratersky, 2016, p. 186.

[80] Orysia Lutsevych and Jon Wallace, "Ukraine-Russia Relations," *Chatham House*, March 24, 2022.

[81] D'Anieri, 2019, pp. 202–203.

[82] D'Anieri, 2019, p. 203.

[83] Charap and Colton, 2017, p. 121.

hold loans and intervene under the claim that it was protecting Ukraine under the 1994 Budapest Memorandum.[84] Russia's failure to shape Ukraine's decisionmaking led Russia to resort to military measures, with the invasion of Crimea and eastern Ukraine and illegal referendum in March 2014 to annex Crimea.

Russia's Actions Leading Up to 2022 Invasion

In the aftermath of Russia's 2014 invasion of eastern Ukraine and illegal annexation of Crimea, Russia continued to use military and non-military means to pursue its goals. Russian media and leadership attacked the legitimacy of Ukraine's 2019 presidential election in the run up to and after the election, including misrepresenting "the findings of international observer missions."[85] Russia also used pro-Russian media owned by pro-Russian Ukrainian oligarchs to portray Kremlin talking points.

Despite these efforts, Russia continued to fail to achieve its objectives in Ukraine, leading to Russia's greater invasion of Ukraine in February 2022. Prevalent among Russian leadership at the time was the perception of Ukrainians perceived lack of will to fight and alleged support for Russia, again demonstrating an inaccurate perception of Ukrainians. Ukrainian opinions of both Putin and Russia had worsened considerably since 2014. Prior to 2014, Putin had a 59 percent approval rating, making him "one of the most popular foreign politicians in Ukraine" and more popular than any Ukrainian politician.[86] In contrast, a November 2019 poll indicated that only 17 percent of Ukrainians had a positive view of Putin, and 71 percent viewed him negatively.[87] Russia's intelligence collection on Ukraine prior to the invasion, however, failed to convey this reality to Russian leadership, despite FSB polling results that indicated "large segments of Ukraine's population were prepared to resist Russian encroachment, and that any expec-

---

[84] D'Anieri, 2019, p. 217.

[85] Hurak and D'Anieri, 2022, p. 126.

[86] Hurak and D'Anieri, 2022, p. 124.

[87] Hurak and D'Anieri, 2022, p. 124.

tation that Russian forces would be greeted as liberators was unfounded."[88] Once again, Russia's actions demonstrated a lack of clear understanding of its neighbor, misguided by Russia's struggle to understand both its identity and that of Ukraine.

---

[88] Greg Miller, Catherine Belton, "Russia's Spies Misread Ukraine and Misled Kremlin as War Loomed," *Washington Post*, August 19, 2022.

CHAPTER 3

Russia's Post-Soviet National Identity and Efforts to Manipulate Ukraine

The previous chapter demonstrates that we should understand Russo-Ukrainian relations as a struggle between two states with the aim of consolidating competing post-Soviet national identities. The West, both through its existence and appeal as a successful model of development and its own integrative institutions, is part of that dynamic. But of greater importance are the choices Russia and Ukraine have made in defining their self-image. Russia, despite some participation in Western initiatives, from the beginning of the post-Soviet period sought to carve out a separate sphere of influence from the greater European project that included Ukraine.

Had Russian political leadership embraced the vision of the westernizers or moderates who saw value in the Western political model of development, there would have been less need for a sphere of influence comprised of countries like Ukraine that were resistant to Russian influence; the outcome of a Ukrainian election, for example, would have been of much less consequence if Russia's vision had been to become a Western country in the mold of, say, Austria (a former seat of empire surrounded by NATO but not a member itself). But the choice of a Western development model required a corresponding identity among Russian elites and the population.

Did this canvas upon which a Western or modern European identity could be formed exist in Russia?[1] Leading Russian reformers in the early

---

[1] Michael Urban, "The Politics of Identity in Russia's Postcommunist Transition: The Nation Against Itself," *Slavic Review*, Vol. 53, No. 3, Autumn 1994.

1990s believed that Russia could become a European country on European terms. But these and other like-minded officials lost the competition for Russia's post-Soviet identity by the late-1990s after a short run at the helm. And because Russia's turn away from the Western model lies at the root of the Russia-Ukraine conflict, we need to understand the reasons for it.

This chapter explores the historical foundations of national identity that post-Soviet Russian leaders and the Russian people inherited from centuries past. Using the elements of national identity presented in Figure 1.2—religious history, unique historical events, and political culture, which help to define national self-image and strategic interests—we show that the outcome of the struggle for Russia's post-Soviet national identity was probably most influenced by cultural and political forces within Russia as opposed to external factors, and the outcome followed a centuries-long pattern in Russian history as an autocratic, non-Western (anti-Western), great power. Those attributes combined to push Russian foreign policy toward seeking control of Ukraine as opposed to following the European path of other former empires on the continent.

Losing Battles of Westernizers in Russian History

Russia's westernizers in the early years of the Russian Federation wanted to create a democracy based on competitive elections, representative government, rule of law, and protection of private property and individual rights. In foreign policy, the idea of Russia as a non-Western, Orthodox great power with unchallenged influence over neighboring Slavs would be replaced with membership in European integrative institutions, which might mitigate any lingering imperial proclivities. There was a place for the CIS, but the guiding light was the West and Russia's new role in it as a constructive partner with a shared vision. Their goals were a deviation from the Russian norm, but the appearance of a westernizing faction—and their subsequent defeat—was not. A version of this reform group has made brief and unsuccessful appearances in Russian history going back to the 1500s.[2]

---

[2] Tsygankov, 2015, p. 7.

The *West* has existed in many forms in Europe over hundreds of years. As a result, what Russian westernizers have tried to achieve has also varied over time. But in general, their primary aim has been to dilute centralized authority, create a more representative government, and protect the property and individual rights of citizens through a more independent judiciary. One of the first instances of pushback against overly consolidated power in Russia came from Prince Andrei Kurbski against Ivan the Terrible in the 16th century.[3] Later, there was the liberal opposition in 1740 during the reign of Elizabeth whose goal was "limiting the powers of the autocracy and curbing the influence of favorites."[4] Sovereigns such as Catherine the Great, Alexander I, and Alexander II rhetorically would endorse initiatives to this end but were supported by much more-influential conservative forces and never allowed power to stray far from the Kremlin.[5]

This pattern has repeated itself in today's Russia. The liberal reformers rather quickly lost influence as their conservative opponents moved Russia back into a familiar place. Among Russian ideologists, "the majority of intellectuals see the broadly defined 'West,' rather than non-Russians of the former Soviet Union, as 'the constituting other' in opposition to which Russian national identity can be forged."[6] In connection with this, many of the same intellectuals predicted that "the inevitable result of this peculiarity will be the recreation of a union on the territory of the USSR [Union of Soviet Socialist Republics]."[7] At the top, Putin in the early 2000s, much like his Tsarist predecessors, used rhetoric about Russian democracy and acceptance of "European integrative processes," while simultaneously undermining the very institutions necessary for a functioning democracy.[8]

Why do Russian westernizers continue to lose battles for national identity in Russian history? Why have they never managed to gain a critical

---

[3] Tsygankov, 2015, p. 7.

[4] Pipes, 2007, p. 72.

[5] Pipes, 2007, p. 80; Hill and Gaddy, 2015, p. 53.

[6] Tolz, 1998, p. 995.

[7] Tolz, 1998, p. 995.

[8] Vladimir Putin, "Annual Address to the Federal Assembly of the Russian Federation," speech, May 26, 2004.

mass of sustained support that would allow for a true shift in national identity in a given era? Fiona Hill and Clifford Gaddy keyed in on the idea that, in Russia, order is often associated with a strong, unchallenged state, while competition for power is seen as destabilizing. According to their account, this was a driving factor for Putin, who, reciting a 19th century Russian philosopher, noted:

> People often think proclaiming various freedoms and universal suffrage will in and of itself have some miraculous strength to direct life onto a new course. In actual fact, in such instances in life, what happens usually turns out not to be democracy, but depending on the turn events take, either oligarchy or anarchy.[9]

In other words, Russian leaders and elite, and to some extent the broader population, tend to advocate or accept autocracy as a strength as opposed to an unwanted imposition.[10] And it has been that way for a long time.[11] Some have pointed to the idea that perhaps this can be explained in part by the arbitrary nature of history and the role of individuals at a given time. Had the reformist politician Boris Nemtsov been elected president instead of Putin, for example, it might have all been different.[12] There could be some truth to this argument, but, given the repetitiveness of the autocratic outcomes in Russia over five centuries, we need to look beyond contemporary circumstances.

The Gravitational Pull of the Past

Following the collapse of the Soviet Union, former Warsaw Pact countries and Soviet republics outside Russia quickly sought to chart their own paths distinct from any association with Moscow. These countries had historical

---

[9] As quoted in Hill and Gaddy, 2015, p. 55.

[10] *Obshchestvennoe mnenie-2014*, Levada-Tsentr, Moscow, 2014, p. 28.

[11] Tsygankov, 2015.

[12] Michael McFaul, "Russia's Road to Autocracy," *Journal of Democracy*, Vol. 32, No. 4, October 2021, p. 17.

precedent they could draw on to pave the way toward a future as independent, European countries. As one scholar wrote, "[a]ll other Eastern European countries could construct their post-communist vision for change in the context of the 'return to Europe' project, viewing Europe as their rightful place of belonging and interpreting their communist past as a forced derailment from their 'normal' historical path."[13] Moreover, nearly all of these societies in Europe were products of the influence of the Catholic and later Protestant faiths and had closer proximity to large centers of economic power and technological innovation, which might have had a positive impact on their ability to transition or return to a democratic, capitalist model of development.[14] In the context of 21st century Europe and its prevailing norms, a return to Europe meant a willingness to integrate on explicit terms of agreement, so underlying historical, cultural, and political conditions might have been important in paving the transition. There was less ambiguity within most of the populations of countries outside Russia that their future lay within the institutions of Europe, even if some citizens did not necessarily identify themselves as European per se.[15]

Russia did not have these precedents to draw on in its search for a post-Soviet identity. In the absence of such alternatives, the gravitational pull of centralized power and an imperial mentality of the Russian empire and Soviet Union would be difficult to overcome.[16] According to Holden, referring to Russian intellectual debates in the early 1990s,

> it became clear that in spite of the democratic and anti-imperial declarations that had contributed to Yeltsin's political victory over the old union/party centre, it was difficult for many Russian intellectuals to

---

[13] Gulnaz Sharafutdinova, *The Red Mirror: Putin's Leadership and Russia's Insecure Identity*, Oxford University Press, 2020, p. 79.

[14] Henrich, 2020; Joel Mokyr, *A Culture of Growth: The Origins of the Modern Economy*, Princeton University Press, 2010.

[15] Michael Bruter, *Citizens of Europe? The Emergence of a Mass European Identity*, Palgrave Macmillan, 2005, p. 166.

[16] Yegor Gaidar, *Collapse of an Empire*, Brookings Institution Press, 2007, p. xiv.

think in terms of a Russian state that was now separated from Ukraine
and [Belarus, and] had lost or was losing its superpower status.[17]

Indeed, Russia began drifting toward its historical political traditions as
early as the mid- to late-1990s. By the early 2000s, Putin began consolidating political control over key aspects of society and, by 2011, had embraced
the narrative of Russia as the leader of a Eurasian counterpart to the EU that
would integrate most of the former Soviet republics, including Ukraine.

Western and Russian observers alike have puzzled over the notion that
Russia over centuries has rejected the prevailing political, economic, and
cultural trends of its more prosperous neighbors to the West. In search of
explanations, experts have returned to what might be called a sticky Russian identity as an autocratic, anti-Western, Orthodox, great power.[18] The
geography of modern Europe combined with Russian insistence that it lead
a distinct bloc of countries, first and foremost Ukraine, who see themselves
as pro-Western or independent European countries, creates conditions that
are difficult to reconcile.[19] To get a grasp of the contradictions, the rest of
this chapter will examine the origins of Russian identity as distinct from
Europe, while the following chapter will explore why Ukraine's identity did
not correspond to that of Russia's.

The Roots of Divergence of Europe and Russia
Religion
There are various theories that could help examine how Russia's sticky
national identity makes transitions to democracy and a market economy

---

[17] Gerard Holden, *Russia After the Cold War: History and the Nation in Post-Soviet
Security Politics*, Westview Press, 1994, p. 164.

[18] Vladimir Baranovsky, "Russia: A Part of Europe or Apart from Europe?" *International Affairs*, Vol. 76, No. 3, July 2000; Dmitry Trenin, "The End of Eurasia: Russia on
the Border Between Geopolitics and Globalization," Carnegie Endowment for International Peace, 2002; Pipes, 2007; Isaiah Berlin, *The Soviet Mind: Russian Culture Under
Communism*, Brookings Institution Press, 2016.

[19] Some scholars were grappling with this question for many years. See, for example,
Samuel Charap, Jeremy Shapiro, and Alyssa Demus, *Rethinking the Regional Order for
Post-Soviet Europe and Eurasia*, RAND Corporation, PE-297-CC/SFDFA, 2018.

a difficult challenge.[20] But one way to explore the question is to look at the divergent developmental histories of Russia and Europe. Using various factors (such as marriage patterns, the role of kinship in community organization, and the transfer of property), a few scholars have zeroed in on the role of the Catholic Church as a key disrupter in human history that played an important role in the development of modern European societies and political systems, which later served as examples that other countries outside Europe have emulated.

The anthropologist Joseph Henrich and others have argued that the sustained presence of Catholicism (and later Protestantism) had a deep impact on European psychology and political development. In brief, the argument is that Catholicism imposed new norms on individuals that were unusual in human history, where people traditionally organized themselves in small clans, and devotion to kin and clan was a primary driver of human behavior and culture. Catholicism's rules unwittingly changed culture such that, over centuries, the individual became more central than the group and kinbased institutions were replaced with those that fostered political, social, and technological change.[21] Greater numbers of people began to travel beyond their communities and form larger cities, marry outside a small network of family members, delay marriage or forego it altogether, question religious dogma, demand greater checks on sovereigns, among others.[22] Making a long story short, these massive changes in human behavior and societal organization, combined with other factors, became the foundation of the democratic political order we know in Europe today.[23]

Fukuyama has similarly argued that such forces were important in creating the "social background to state building in Europe." With kinship on the wane as a binding element of community, feudalism took its place, and, over time, this "made a huge difference to the subsequent political development

---

[20] Daniel Ziblatt, "How Did Europe Democratize," *World Politics*, Vol. 58, No. 2, January 2006.

[21] Fukuyama, 2011, pp. 229–241.

[22] Henrich, p. 471; J. Hajnal, "European Marriage Patterns in Perspective," in D. V. Glass and D. E. C. Eversley, eds., *Population in History: Essays in Historical Demography*, Edward Arnold LTD, 1965, pp. 101–143.

[23] Fukuyama, 2011.

of Europe."[24] This societal undergirding made it easier for the appearance of what we understand today as the rule of law and accountable government. Fukuyama goes on to detail the ways in which certain groups in Western Europe, freed from the restrictions of kin-centric norms (among other factors), were, over time, able to establish themselves as wealthy, independent political forces to be reckoned with by central authorities. As a result,

> ... few [European] rulers felt free simply to confiscate private property without legal cause. As a consequence, they did not have unlimited taxing authority and needed to borrow money from bankers to finance their wars. European aristocrats were also more secure in their persons against arbitrary arrest or execution. Apart from in Russia, European monarchs refrained from launching campaigns of outright terror and intimidation against the elites in their societies.[25]

How is this relevant to Russia? The Russian Federation traces its religious origins to the acceptance of Orthodox Christianity by Vladimir in Kyiv in 988. One might assume that outcomes in Russia should have been similar given the seeming closeness of these Christian religions. But Fukuyama points out that the "Eastern church in Constantinople [from which Russian Orthodoxy traces its origins] made no parallel effort to change marriage and inheritance laws."[26] So far as we know, there is to date insufficient research on the Russian Orthodox Church's influence on family and societal norms and whether those influences were important to Russia's political development.

What evidence there is lends plausibility to the idea that there was some divergence in norms and outcomes between the Catholic and Russian Orthodox Churches. Using the indicator of marriage patterns, Hanjal, in 1965, noted that marriage patterns in Russia were distinct from Western Europe. Hanjal showed that in Western Europe there was a pattern of "high age at marriage" and a relatively large proportion who never married at all. He noted, "the 'European' pattern pervaded the whole of Europe except for

---

[24] Fukuyama, 2011, pp. 238–240.

[25] Fukuyama, 2011, p. 323.

[26] Fukuyama, 2011, p. 241.

the eastern and south-eastern portion."[27] When scholars, following up on Hanjal's research, took a closer look at Russian family structures in the mid-18th century compared with those of Central Europe, they found a more "rigid [patrilineal] structure of the household, restricted to the pure family unit."[28] Delaying of marriage, particularly by women, or having a more fluid family structure is an indication that long-standing patterns of behavior and family structure—observed most everywhere else in the world as of a few hundred years ago—had somehow been disrupted in Europe, where the individual was taking center stage. This matters because the drivers of the social foundation for the particular political change that took place in Europe might have been absent in Russia for much longer.

It could be that the Catholic Church is not the right determinant of such behavior. Perhaps Europeans and Russians were responding less to the requirements of their churches and more to the exigencies of their respective environments, as Pipes has emphasized.[29] But there do appear to be important differences in the societal and psychological evolution of Europe from most other places in the world, which might have, over time, led to different political, social, and economic outcomes. And these outcomes—system of governance, economic model, protection of individual rights—have become a means to differentiate members from non-members in 21st century Europe.

To be sure, this theory only tries to account for the roots of European psychology that were more likely to embrace democracy and market economies. Clearly the path was different for various European societies along the way, and there were hard turns away from it at times, such as with Nazi Germany.[30] There are also the examples of Asian countries such as South Korea and Taiwan, who, after decades of authoritarian rule and entirely separate cultural and political histories from Europe, successfully transitioned to democracy. But for Europe, the psychological and cultural groundwork

---

[27] Hajnal, 1965, p. 101.

[28] Michael Mitterauer and Alexander Kagan, "Russian and Central European Family Structures: A Comparative View," *Journal of Family History*, Spring 1982, p. 127.

[29] Richard Pipes, *Russia Under the Old Regime*, 2nd ed., Penguin Books, 1997.

[30] Ziblat, 2006, p. 312.

for democracy might have been laid by unique changes imposed by arbitrary and particular rules of the Catholic Church, and, from there, emulation became a choice of individual countries outside Europe based on their own cultural evolution and resultant national identity.

Russia's conversion to Orthodoxy in the 10th century was consequential in other ways. It created and continues to create a mechanism for Russians to distinguish themselves from much of the rest of Europe (with the exception of majorities in Ukraine, Belarus, Bulgaria, and other southeastern European countries), whose religious roots over the past 1,000 years or more trace to Catholicism and later Protestantism. According to a 2001 Levada poll, for example, 71 percent of Russian citizens surveyed agreed that Russia "belonged to a special—'Eurasian' or Orthodox—civilization and as a result a western course of development was not appropriate [for Russia]."[31] Many of the prevailing Russian political identities we described in Chapter 1 similarly emphasize that Russia should not follow the Western path or be integrated into European institutions, in part because of its distinct Slavic, Orthodox heritage.[32]

Finally, there is discussion that the Orthodox religion played another role in the development of Russian political culture. Pipes has argued that Russian Orthodoxy—in addition to geographical and external factors (i.e., the Mongol occupation)—in its relation to political development inherited its norms from Byzantium as opposed to Catholicism.[33] This meant there was less expectation of the monarchy to act in the interest of the subjects. In turn, in Russia, "a form of monarchy [emerged] that in its powers exceeded anything known in the West even in the age of absolutism."[34] Fukuyama makes a similar point on a more general level that religion can play a pivotal role in checking the power of the sovereign.[35]

Although it is a complex question regarding how and why this all transpired in Russia, a general identity that accepted highly centralized and

---

[31] Levada Center, "Press-vypusk No. 32: 13 noiabria 2001 goda," November 13, 2001.

[32] Clunan, 2009.

[33] Pipes, 2007, p. 13.

[34] Pipes, 2007, p. 13.

[35] Fukuyama, 2011, p. 241.

unchallenged authority without political competition, a free press, an independent judiciary, or full property rights generally has persisted as the Russian/Soviet model for hundreds of years, up to 1991. Indeed, in the Putin era there has been a mutually reinforcing relationship between autocracy (Putin) and the Orthodox Church. The state protects the church, and the church protects the state.[36]

One obvious issue with this line of argument is that Ukraine itself is predominantly an Orthodox country and yet seems somewhat more receptive to the Western development model. While this is true, Ukraine has a more complex (or simply different) political landscape than Russia, perhaps because of the forces described above. Western Ukraine in particular has some shared history with Catholic Poland, for example, and that part of Ukraine has been vocal and participatory in charting a Western course for their country. There are other differences that we explore in more detail in the next chapter. The broader point is that the Orthodox faith in and of itself might not be determinant of anything, but when we consider other research on the role of the Catholic Church in setting conditions for European political development, it seems fair to raise this argument that Eastern Orthodoxy, combined with other unique factors in Russian history (see next section), might have been influential in Russia's case.

Unique Historical Events

While parts of Europe were slowly undergoing psychological and cultural change in the Middle Ages, Russians from the late 1200s to the 1400s were living, to some degree, under Mongol rule and were largely isolated from the changes underway in Europe. The Mongols departed and Russians, after defeating more-democratic leaning principalities such as Novgorod, retained an extreme political model buttressed by a religion that, apparently, contributed neither the individualistic nor political outcomes found in Europe.

To be sure, Russia, for centuries, in some respects resembled many other monarchies in Europe. According to Poe,

---

[36] Carlo J. V. Caro, "Vladimir Putin's 'Orthodoxy, Autocracy, and Nationality," Center for Ethics and the Rule of Law, University of Pennsylvania, August 31, 2022.

> Muscovy [1547–1721] was, despite its peculiarities, a monarchy of common early modern type: Russia was ruled by a king, who was simultaneously the head of a dynastic family, the chief prince of a central court, and the titular lord of a large territorial state...the Russian governing class worked in institutions that were similar to those all over Europe . . . .[37]

At the same time, European observers of Russia who had expertise in the workings of political mechanisms of their time "spoke with one voice: royal authority was far more extensive in Russia than anywhere else in Europe."[38] Examples of this, according to various accounts, were the inability of seemingly comparable institutions in Russia to check the power of the tsar; the lack of protections of private property; and the ability of the Russian sovereign to infringe upon the liberty of citizens, particularly the nobility.[39] Some thoughtful Russian observers of the system viewed these traits of the Russian system as most appropriate for Russia. As Nikolai Karamzin, a Russian historian, stated around 1810, "Autocracy has founded and resuscitated Russia. Any change in her political constitution has led in the past and must lead in the future to her perdition."[40]

In his study of Russian political culture, Pipes pointed to three factors that distinguished Russia from Europe. We discussed two of these above—the influence of Mongol occupation to the 15th century and the ways in which the Orthodox church might have shaped Russia's culture and the relationship between sovereign and subject. The third factor is the way in which the Russian state originated. According to Pipes, geography in a variety of ways inhibited the development of important institutions that, over time, allowed Europeans to challenge and dilute central authority. The lack of natural boundaries and the immense territory led to a situation in which "medieval Russia lacked the two institutions that in the West served to limit the power of kings: an independent nobility and middle class, and private

---

[37] Marshall T. Poe, *"A People Born to Slavery": Russia in Early Modern European Ethnography, 1476–1748,* Cornell University Press, 2000, p. 201.

[38] Poe, 2000, p. 203.

[39] Poe, 2000, p. 201; Pipes, 2007, p. 8.

[40] As cited in Pipes, 2007, p. 1.

property in land."[41] Tsygankov made a similar argument, noting that "state relationships with the elites and an intense security dilemma" paved the path to Russian autocracy.[42]

The security assertion is difficult to accept given the number of countries that have found ways to democratize and integrate in Europe despite long histories of invasion. Regardless, the end result in Russia was a society that was unable or unwilling to mobilize a critical mass of support to challenge highly centralized authority. Once this baseline was established, for whatever reason, an identity took hold among influential elites that unchecked authority was Russia's natural condition and, moreover, this condition was the foundation of Russian greatness.

Post-Soviet Russia's Continuity in Political Culture and National Identity

Time and again in Russian history, consolidated, unchallenged power has proved the norm. The justifications for the need for change, though they tend to revolve around the idea that Russia is weak, vulnerable to disintegration, and exploited by external powers when there is a competitive political environment within Russia. It could be that religion, geography, and unique historical experiences have determined Russia's cultural and psychological tendencies, which influence the adoption of a national identity as an autocratic, Orthodox, non-Western great power. More research needs to be done to investigate this hypothesis.

In any case, the gravitational pull of the past is not absolute. It is possible for countries to break out of patterns of behavior and a previous national identity. Europe's transition itself was neither simple nor quick, and the citizens and elite of former empires have come to accept a new identity as prosperous members of the European order.[43] The Asia-Pacific region presents several interesting cases of transition to democracy. Taiwan, Malaysia, and South Korea demonstrate that the influence of the Catholic Church and the cultural changes it wrought were not a prerequisite for an authoritarian

---

[41] Pipes, 2007, p. 11.

[42] Tsygankov, 2015, p. 7.

[43] Ziblatt, 2006.

country to embrace a new political culture with greater division of power in the 20th and 21st centuries.[44] The rise of democracy in Europe from the 19th century to present accompanied by higher standards of living probably increased the appeal to emulate the Western model. And Russia meets many of the benchmarks scholars have highlighted in more-recent transitions to democracy: high education levels, high urban populations, and economic growth throughout the 2000s (since moving into stagnation). But the continuity of Russian national identity as described shows that the past is powerful, and that change should not be a baseline expectation.

As soon as it became clear that westernizing reformers in post-Soviet Russia were not going to be able to perform economic miracles overnight, conservative forces with tendencies toward centralized authority and expansionary foreign policy gradually took over, reverting to centuries of tradition. In 1993, the Russian parliament, in the midst of a power struggle with the Kremlin, voted 160 to 0 to declare sovereignty over Sevastopol, the home of the former Soviet Black Sea Fleet in Crimea, Ukraine.[45] Yeltsin vetoed the measure, but Russia, in these early post-Soviet years, was promoting the CIS as a mechanism of "integration" of states in the former Soviet space whose populations had just voted overwhelmingly in favor of independence from Moscow's previous attempt at uniting eastern Europe and Central Asia under its control. Ukraine signed on but was never truly interested in the project; Georgia declined outright insisting, according to Kozyrev, that "the independence of [Georgia] needed no confirmation and that the CIS represented too great an integration with Russia and the other former Soviet republics."[46]

In the 1990s, researchers were interested in examining the degree to which Russian views on the most appropriate form of governance were changing. The results were mixed; some studies suggested there were

[44] Rafiq Dossani, Eugeniu Han, Cortez A. Cooper III, and Sale Lilly, *Democracy in the Asia-Pacific Region*, RAND Corporation, RR-A1515-1, 2021, pp. 15–19; James Cotton, "From Authoritarianism to Democracy in South Korea," *Political Studies*, Vol. 37, No. 2, 1989.

[45] "Yeltsin Assails Parliament Vote Claiming Crimean Port for Russia," 1993.

[46] Andrei Kozyrev, *The Fire Bird: The Elusive Fate of Russian Democracy*, University of Pittsburgh Press, 2019, pp. 54–55.

grounds to expect Russia's democratic tradition to be sustainable.[47] Others were more cautious on the prospects of what would have been a sea change in Russian political traditions, arguing there was an important difference between subjective views of democracy and actual political behavior of both the general public and elites.[48] Russian behavior in the succeeding years showed the apprehension was appropriate.

In 1995, Sergei Karaganov, a member of the "statists" or "moderate conservatives" welcomed the departure of Andrei Kozyrev as foreign minister, writing, "in his successors [the Americans] will face Russian politicians whose policies are based on national interest, not ideological friendship or hatred."[49] In 1996, the "old apparatchiks in the bureaucracy, especially in the military-security apparatus, wanted: to do little more than change the communist red banner to the new tricolor flag over the Kremlin" retained considerable sway in Russian politics.[50] Specifically, by the middle of the 1990s, "the balance of power between liberal reformers and their critics in the new parliament . . . became relatively equal."[51] Others found that, in fact, as early as 1992, "a certain advantage seems to have passed to the [Russian] right wing."[52] The argument in 1998 by Andrei Kokoshin, the secretary of the Russian Security Council from 1992 to 1996, that the future of global politics would largely depend on the outcome of Russia's relations with Ukraine, showed that senior Russian officials were still thinking about Russia's role in its immediate neighborhood and not about Russia's place in greater Europe through a transformation into a democratic stakeholder on the continent.[53]

---

[47] Fleron, 1996; John T. Ishiyama, Michael K. Launer, Irina E. Likhachova, David Cratis Williams, and Marilyn J. Young, "Russian Electoral Politics and the Search for National Identity," *Argumentation and Advocacy*, Vol. 34, No. 2, 1997.

[48] Fleron, 1996.

[49] Sergei Karaganov, "Russia and the West After Kozyrev," Project Syndicate, September 2, 1995.

[50] Kozyrev, 2019, p. 124.

[51] McFaul, 2021, p. 16.

[52] Urban, 1992, p. 12.

[53] Andrei A. Kokoshin, *Soviet Strategic Thought, 1917–91*, MIT Press, 1998, p. 198.

The die for post-Soviet national identity was probably cast by the mid-to-late 1990s. But the nail in the coffin for Russian reformers occurred in 2002–2003, before NATO expansion became a more existential issue in senior Russian rhetoric.[54] That is the time when President Putin began to consolidate control over the Russian state.[55] Ownership of key media and energy companies transferred into the hands of the state or those who would be loyal to the Kremlin. Since that time, political opposition has been muzzled, and Russia's legislative bodies and judiciary are not independent. Laws have been repeatedly changed to allow Putin to remain in the presidency practically for life. Power has become centralized in the hands of Putin and loyal associates. In Freedom House's measure of the level of democratic governance of 29 countries from Central Europe to Central Asia, Russia is classified as a "consolidated authoritarian regime," with a democracy score just above Tajikistan, Belarus, and Uzbekistan.[56]

There were implications of Russia's "road to autocracy" for Russian foreign policy. The sharp turn away from democracy meant a separate sphere of influence outside the EU, which some of Russia's neighbors aspired to join. In 2011, in the lead-up to his return to the presidency, Putin promoted the idea of a Eurasian Union as a counterpart to the EU. The Eurasian Union was essentially a plan to integrate the former Soviet space, excluding Estonia, Latvia, and Lithuania. This was a decision based on an identity for Russia as, if not an anti-Western country, a non-Western country that did not share the same vision as much of the rest of Europe. Indeed, even Russia's closest neighbors were unlikely to sign on willingly. As Marlene Laruelle, a leading scholar on Russia and Eurasianism, asked even before Putin advocated this idea, "What could [countries such as Ukraine, Moldova, Georgia, and Azerbaijan] really want to share [with Russia]? . . . The political elites [of these countries] have no interest reconstituting any supranational entity.

---

[54] Clint Reach, "The Origins of Russian Conduct," *PRISM*, Vol. 9, No. 3, November 2021, p. 4.

[55] Karen Dawisha, *Putin's Kleptocracy: Who Owns Russia?* Simon & Schuster, 2015, pp. 273–278.

[56] Freedom House, "Countries and Territories. Democracy Scores," webpage, undated.

The Georgia-Ukraine-Azerbaijan-Moldova affiliation [known as GUAM] was the first prototype of an 'anti-Russian Eurasia . . . .'"[57]

In the 19th and 20th centuries, Russia's form of governance did not preclude making common cause against rising threats to the balance of power in Europe. Russia joined other European powers to put down the French threat of the early 19th century. It formed an alliance with France in the late 19th century to protect against a growing German threat. Russia later made a pact with Germany in the interwar period, unsuccessfully hedging against the possibility of a war with Germany after Munich in 1938. And it fought alongside the Allies after Germany reneged on the agreement. With virtual consensus across Europe on political, economic, and military matters, Russia as an autocratic great power has very little room to maneuver to find common cause with other European countries. In today's Europe, Russia has the greatest success in alliance-building with other autocratic countries such as Belarus and, up until early 2022, Kazakhstan.

Place of Ukraine in Russian National Identity

There was an important link between Russian adoption of a Euro-centric national identity and peace with Ukraine. This is because, as noted several times in this report, all other political factions in Russia retained an imperial mindset and were adamant about Russia's post-Soviet role in the near abroad, in particular in Ukraine and Belarus. In fact, even some leading Russian reformers were not prepared to let go of Russia's historical claims on Crimea.[58] This was also true for many Russian citizens. According to Tolz in 1998, "many Russians prefer nation building to take place around their own culture and language. Ukrainians and Belarussians are regarded as sharing this culture and values. Therefore, many Russians are ready to accept them as part of the Russian nation."[59] Of course, political groups such as the Communists and Eurasianists were prepared to go beyond "acceptance" as part of the Russian nation (see Figure 3.1, a map used in an article on a new-Eurasianist website). In other words, as soon as Russia turned toward a more

---

[57] Marlène Laruelle, *Russian Eurasianism: Ideology of Empire*, Johns Hopkins University Press, 2012, p. 218.

[58] D'Anieri, 2018, p. 10.

[59] Tolz, 1998, p. 1018.

FIGURE 3.1

Neo-Eurasianist Vision for the Partition of Ukraine

SOURCE: Reproduced from Nicholas Nicholaides, "Russia Needs Novorossiya," Geopolitica.ru, October 18, 2017.

traditional national identity, away from the protective umbrella of a shared European vision, there was a real chance for confrontation and violence in Ukraine. And Russia began moving in this direction as early as the mid-to-late 1990s, just a few years after the collapse of the Soviet Union.

If Russia is a distinct entity from the West and it is a great power, then it needs a separate sphere of influence. That sphere of influence could be based on a common threat or some other common interest. In the view of many Russian elites and the population, the threat is the encroachment of Western political and social culture, and the common interest is the perpetuation of a Russian identity based on a perceived shared culture, history, language, and religion with Belarus and Ukraine. This is why Lieven warned in the late 1990s of the risks of a divergence of Russian and Ukrainian post-Soviet national identity. And it is why Trenin, in light of Ukrainian independence in 1991, urged, "it [is] imperative that Russia find a new identity and a new international role" from its previous one as leader of the Orthodox Slavs.[60]

Putin's rhetoric around the Crimea annexation and the large-scale invasion of Ukraine was an unmistakable marker of Russia's complete "breakout from the post–Cold War system."[61] And the reason for this was Russia's reversion to an identity that left Russia seeking a leading role based on this particular self-image in a region with contrary identities and national aspirations. To put a finer point on it, Russian post-1991 national identity became wholly incompatible not only with European institutions but with Ukraine, the majority of whose citizens rejected Putin's proclamation in 2014 that "[Russia and Ukraine] are not simply close neighbors but . . . one people. Kiev is the mother of Russian cities. Ancient Rus' is our common source and we cannot live without each other."[62]

Conclusion

Had Russia embraced a different national identity, a Russian president would not have addressed the Russian parliament with a speech justifying the illegal annexation of Crimea with the statement that Russia and Ukraine are "one people." But the gravitational pull of the past proved to be too strong to overcome. Indeed, the prevailing political forces in Russia had no interest in adopting such an identity because they believed it was not optimal for Russia. Nikolai Karamzin's 1810 opinion that change in Russia's "political constitution . . . must lead in the future to her perdition" carried through to the leaders of the post-Soviet period. Were it not for centuries of similar political outcomes in Russia, we could chalk up Russia's political path to particularities of the time, individuals and their choices that could have gone another way. But Russia continues to end up in the same place, and that, in our view, is probably the result of religious and unique

---

[60] Trenin, 2002, p. 96.

[61] Dmitri Trenin, "Russia's Breakout from the 'Post-Cold War System,'" Carnegie Moscow Center, 2013.

[62] President of Russia, "Address by President of Russian Federation," press release, March 18, 2014.

historical factors that perpetuate an identity of autocracy, Orthodoxy, and anti-Westernism.

Given Russia's imperial past, and little interest in giving it up among key parts of the Russian polity, Russian reversion to its traditional identity had clear implications for Ukraine. Once it was clear that Russia would not be a part of Europe in the form of Austria, for instance, the preexisting beliefs about Russia as a great power with a privileged interest in its near abroad came to the fore. Thus, Russia sought to drag its neighbor—which Putin asserted in 2022 and before was not a real country—into a relationship that unsurprisingly was irreconcilable with Ukraine's national identity and aspirations.[63]

On the surface, what is remarkable about Russia-Ukraine relations over the past 30 years is that such a violent rupture could have occurred. Ukraine, despite events such as the Holodomor (the famine caused by Stalin's policies in the early 1930s that killed millions), might have been more receptive to Russian entreaties than it was. Ukraine is also a predominantly Orthodox country with a Slavic language located on the outer edges of Europe without the aforementioned prerequisites commonly found in countries that aspire to the Western model of development. While Ukraine did share many of the same challenges as Russia in its post-Soviet political and economic evolution, Ukraine, at first politely and then forcefully, rejected the Russian vision. Belarus, to date, has taken a different approach. Ukraine has shown that it is different, and we need to investigate why to understand the origins of the war.

---

[63] President of Russia, "Address by the President of the Russian Federation," press release, February 21, 2022.

CHAPTER 4

Ukrainian National Identity and Resistance to Russian Manipulation

Introduction

In public remarks justifying Russia's 2022 invasion of Ukraine, President Putin repeatedly cited the neighboring countries' mutual history, shared kinship, and "spiritual unity."[1] Just three days before the first missiles rained down over Ukrainian territory in 2022, he stated, "I would like to emphasize again that Ukraine is not just a neighboring country for us. It is an inalienable part of our own history, culture and spiritual space."[2] In several instances, the Kremlin leader has denied the very existence of a unique Ukrainian identity. This narrative claiming that Ukraine and Russia are inextricably linked via a longstanding brotherhood is one the Kremlin has embraced throughout the post–Cold War period, particularly since its annexation of Crimea and incursions into the Donbas in 2014. It is one that also alleges the growing rift between Russians and Ukrainians has been knowingly manufactured by the West and neo-Nazis in Kyiv.[3] In Putin's own words roughly six months prior to the invasion,

---

[1] President of Russia, "On the Historical Unity of Russians and Ukrainians," press release, July 12, 2021.

[2] President of Russia, 2022.

[3] President of Russia, 2022.

the wall that has emerged in recent years between Russia and Ukraine, between parts of what is essentially the same historical and spiritual space, to my mind is our great common misfortune and tragedy. These are, first and foremost, the consequences of our own mistakes made at different periods of time. But these are also the result of deliberate efforts by those forces that have always sought to undermine our unity . . . the overarching goal being to divide and then to pit the parts of a single people against one another.[4]

Yet despite these alleged bonds binding Russia and Ukraine, developments since late February 2022 point to a fundamental misunderstanding of Ukrainian national identity by the Kremlin. As we now know based on accounts that surfaced in the first weeks of the war, when the first wave of Russian soldiers set foot on Ukrainian soil on February 24 and the first salvos of missiles struck Kyiv, Russian forces were surprised when met with stiff resistance.[5] Instead of the warm welcome they were reportedly told to expect from "liberated" Ukrainians, Russian soldiers were described by many Ukrainians as "occupiers," "enemies," and "fascists."[6] These reactions, and elements of the Russian Ministry of Defense's operational planning, suggest that Russian civilian and military leaders overlooked several foundational features of Ukraine's national journey and the evolution of its national identity.

The history of the Ukrainian people is one marked by countless annexations and occupations, shifting boundaries, and marginalization. Western historians cite the territory's expansive steppes, nutrient-rich soil, natural resources, and absence of topographical barriers as major contributing factors to this fate. Journalist Anna Reid distills some of this complex history noting, "Ukraine was split between Russia and Poland from the mid seventeenth century to the end of the eighteenth, between Russia and Austria through the nineteenth, and between Russia, Poland, Czechoslovakia, and

---

[4] President of Russia, 2022.

[5] Célia Belin, James Goldgeier, Steven Pifer, and Angela Stent, "Russia's Ambitions, Ukraine's Resistance, and the West's Response," *Brookings*, March 28, 2022.

[6] "Ukrainian Woman Offers Seeds to Russian Soldiers So 'Sunflowers Grow When They Die'," *The Guardian*, February 25, 2022.

Romania between the two world wars."[7] These centuries-long struggles have etched a deep imprint on the Ukrainian psyche, shaping the development of the modern-day Ukrainian identity, cultural narratives, and national symbols. For instance, the Ukrainian people's bloody experiences at the hands of the Tsarist, Soviet, and now post-Soviet regimes, have shaped the Ukrainian identity such that it has been defined, at least in part, by rejecting what Ukrainian identity is not—it is not Russian, nor is it a facsimile of Russia.[8]

Despite the fact that Ukraine gained its independence in 1991, it struggled to form a cohesive national identity for the first two decades of the post–Cold War period.[9] For much of this era the question of what independence would mean in practice was contested among Ukrainian political blocs—a fissure that Russia continuously attempted to exploit.[10] Should Ukraine embrace its between-ness (Russia, Soviet Union, Asia, and Europe) and find its own unique way, or is Ukraine destined to make a choice between these two identities? Should Ukraine focus on using its long-awaited chance to rebuild its oppressed culture and traditions, even if it might mean some internal tensions, or should it prioritize the reforms and build a prosperous society as it might serve as a unifying factor for a nation that has been torn apart for so long?

Each major political upheaval in Ukraine, and Russia's subsequent attempts to shape the outcome, has been followed by increased cohesion in Ukrainian national identity as independent from Russia. Evidence indicates that Russia's 2022 invasion of Ukraine was a profound motivating factor in this respect, spurring the consolidation of a Ukrainian national identity around pillars that are not favorable to Russian interests.[11] Ukraine's linguistic divisions have faded, support for an independent state has grown, unfavorable views of the Russian government have swelled, and the Ukrai-

---

[7] Anna Reid, *Borderland: A Journey Through the History of Ukraine*, Basic Books, 2015, p. I.

[8] Leonid Kuchma, *Ukraine Is Not Russia [Україна — не Росія]*, Vremia, 2004.

[9] Oles' Donii, *Transformation of the Ukrainian National Idea [Трансформація української національної ідеї]*, Nash Format, 2020, p. 9.

[10] Donii, 2020.

[11] Ishaan Tharoor, "How Russia's Invasion Strengthened Ukrainian Identity," *Washington Post*, August 24, 2022.

nian public's desire to join European institutions has grown.[12] This is to say that, by virtue of its skewed conception of Ukrainian identity, recent Kremlin behavior designed to narrow the gap between Russia and Ukraine has widened it.

To recall, in Chapter 1 we outlined the framework we adopted for our analysis of Ukrainian national identity, which includes the ideas of content, contestation, and intensity. After describing each in greater detail in the Ukraine case, we characterize the core characteristics of the Ukrainian identity, limiting our discussion to Ukraine's post-Soviet identity. We close with a discussion of the role of these dynamics in the origins of the ongoing conflict.

Ukrainian Culture, Historical Ties, Language

What features do we have in common that unite us? This is the foundational question associated with the *constitutive norms* of a group's collective identity. This refers to the defining attributes that determine group membership; the traits and unique practices that shape the boundaries of that particular group. In other words, what are the features that make Ukrainians *Ukrainian*?

This is a challenging question to answer parsimoniously for several reasons. As we explain in the section on contestation below, organic and artificial fissures dividing Ukrainians have long existed and been exploited, including in the post–Cold War period. Moreover, Ukrainian national identity has evolved in the thirty-plus years since the collapse of the Soviet Union. Thus, the answer to what makes someone Ukrainian is a matter of both perspective and time—for much of the post–Cold War era, those hailing from eastern Ukraine would likely have had a somewhat distinct conception of "being Ukrainian" than would their fellow countrymen from the west. But Russia's invasions in 2014 and particularly 2022 have narrowed the gap between differing conceptions of Ukrainian identity, resulting in a more homogenous one. We explain these dynamics below.

Having been deprived of their own state for centuries, Ukrainians focused on the preservation of their culture and traditions that served as a

---

[12] Rating Group, 2022a; Rating Group, 2022b; and Rating Group, 2022c.

foundation for their sense of belonging.[13] After the dissolution of the Soviet Union, Ukraine struggled to define the foundations upon which a new nation could be built. Although most of the population supported independence, varying perspectives on who Ukrainians were and what path their state should pursue were contested.

Yet, cultural hallmarks did not serve as a unifying factor for the newly independent Ukraine given that divergent regional approaches to Ukraine's history, present, and future surfaced and began to dominate the national agenda. Competing conceptions of Ukrainian identity based on discrepant historical memories, religion, culture, and language divided Ukraine.[14] At least four groups could be distinguished based on language alone: Ukrainian-speaking Ukrainians, Ukrainian-speaking Russians (a very small part of the population but still present), Russian-speaking Ukrainians, and Russian-speaking Russians.[15] The new country's population was divided among four dominant religions, three Orthodox churches and one Ukrainian Greek Catholic Church (also known as Uniate).[16] Likewise, the history of the Ukrainian people was contested, and intense debates on the impact of specific historic personalities or events on Ukraine's path to independence were highly polarizing.[17]

Interestingly, polls suggest that in the first decades of their independence Ukrainians largely defined themselves along neutral, civic lines rather than by more divisive ethnic and cultural markers, language, or other historic features. For instance, when asked "what makes someone a Ukrainian," in a national 1998 survey, the most prevalent answer selected by respondents was "consciousness of oneself as a Ukrainian" (40.4 percent).[18] Sig-

---

[13] Kulyk, 2016a.

[14] Yaroslav Hrytsak, "National Identities in Post-Soviet Ukraine: The Case of Lviv and Donetsk," *Harvard Ukrainian Studies,* Vol. 22, 1998.

[15] Hrytsak, 1998, p. 263.

[16] Andrew Wilson, "Elements of a Theory of Ukrainian Ethno-National Identities," *Nations and Nationalism*, Vol. 8, No. 1, 2002.

[17] Serhii Plokhy, "The Ghosts of Pereyaslav: Russo-Ukrainian Historical Debates in the Post-Soviet Era," *Europe-Asia Studies*, Vol. 53, No. 3, 2001.

[18] Wilson, 2002.

nificantly fewer respondents selected "Ukrainian ancestors" (22.7 percent), "consciousness of Ukraine's separate history," (4.9 percent) or "the Ukrainian language" (3.9 percent).[19] Despite some differences over foreign policy choices, predominately inclusivist attitudes toward citizenship and support for independence in these early years can serve as an indication of an emerging political nation in Ukraine.[20]

These trends continued in the 2000s. A 2001 survey by the Ukrainian Centre for Economic and Political Studies confirmed the prevalence of this civic-based understanding of Ukraine's national identity.[21] When asked to identify the qualities which make a person "a real member of Ukrainian society," most respondents selected: respecting laws and political institutions; being a citizen of Ukraine; considering Ukraine one's homeland. More ethnic-oriented traits, such as language or religion, were far less prevalent.[22] While two competing versions of Ukraine's *ethnic* national identity—an ethnic Ukrainian national identity and an Eastern Slavic national identity—remained salient in this period, the country's united civic national identity played an increasingly important role.[23] In fact, it appears to have been a driving force behind the democratic reforms and the 2004 protests (the Orange Revolution).[24]

This readiness to unite on the basis of civic identity increased even further after the Revolution of Dignity (2013–2014), Russia's annexation of Crimea, and its first invasion of Ukraine in 2014. A survey conducted by major Ukrainian polling organizations in 2017 showed a drastic increase

---

[19] Ihor Stebelsky, "Ethnic Self-Identification in Ukraine, 1989–2001: Why More Ukrainians and Fewer Russians?" *Canadian Slavonic Papers*, Vol. 51. No, 1, March 2009, p. 99; Wilson, 2002.

[20] William Zimmerman, "Is Ukraine a Political Community?" *Communist and Post-Communist Studies,* Vol. 31, No. 1, 1998.

[21] Stephen Shulman, "The Contours of Civic and Ethnic National Identification in Ukraine," *Europe-Asia Studies,* Vol. 56, No. 1, January 1, 2004.

[22] Shulman, 2004.

[23] Shulman, 2004.

[24] Taras Kuzio, "Nationalism, Identity and Civil Society in Ukraine: Understanding the Orange Revolution," *Communist and Post-Communist Studies,* Vol. 43, No. 3, September 1, 2010.

in the number of those who self-identified as Ukrainians across all regions and age groups.[25] In 2022, 95 percent of respondents chose this response. Although this last number is likely affected by the displacement of Ukrainians because of Russia's full-scale invasion, scholars have argued that Russia's invasion significantly strengthened Ukraine's national identity.[26]

Relational Comparisons–Features That Differentiate Ukrainians from Others

Group identities are not only defined by the traits they do possess, but also by those they do not. Here the fundamental questions are, "what features do we have in common that distinguish us from other . . . communities?" and "how do our common traits relate us to other nations?"[27] With respect to nations in particular, Shulman notes that

> members of a nation often define their "in-group" not only in contrast, but also in *opposition*, to a foreign "out-group." In this case, the out-group serves as a negative reference group for the in-group. . It is also possible for an out-group to serve as a positive reference group, however.[28]

For Ukrainian national identity, Russia and Russians have generally served as the former, the out-group against which many Ukrainians differentiate themselves against, particularly in the post–Cold War period.[29] As we explain below, the Ukrainian identity is not homogenous. While we argue that the degree of *contestation* within Ukrainian national identity has diminished over the course of the post–Cold War period, particularly in the

---

[25] Myroslav Chekh and Ihor Hryniv, "The National Question: Ukraine as Europe" ["Національне питання: Україна як Європа"], *Mirror Weekly*, June 17, 2017.

[26] Alexander J. Motyl, "The Language of Russia's War on Ukraine," *Foreign Policy*, March 13, 2022.

[27] Stephen Shulman, "The Cultural Foundations of Ukrainian National Identity," *Ethnic and Racial Studies*, Vol. 22, No. 6, November 1999, p. 1014.

[28] Shulman, 1999, p. 1014.

[29] Denys Kiryukhin, "Roots and Features of Modern Ukrainian National Identity and Nationalism," *E-International Relations*, March 19, 2015, p. 60.

past decade, variation still exists. At some points in recent history, in certain pockets of Ukraine, views toward Russia, Russians, and Ukraine's relationship with Moscow have been largely positive. Moreover, evidence indicates that Ukrainians have been torn on the question of orientation—whether to look east versus west when defining national identity. In this sense, Russia has not exclusively served as the "other" against which to define Ukrainian national identity (see section on contestation below for additional details). As scholar Taras Kuzio notes, the "sense of 'Otherness' becomes more urgent when two sides are both ethnically close and where one nationality refuses to recognize the separate existence of the 'Other'."[30] In other words, Kuzio argues that Russia's unyielding refusal to recognize the Ukrainian people, language, culture, and state as distinct has actually contributed to the crystallization of a Ukrainian identity around the shared attribute of being "not Russian."[31]

Why is it that Russia, of all the external powers who occupied what is present-day Ukraine, has emerged as the other in Ukrainian national identity? The answer lies, at least in part, in the seeds planted early in the neighbors' historic relationship. As we discuss above, Ukrainian and Russian history have long been entwined, predating the establishment of the Russian empire in 1721. Both nations, for instance, cite the medieval-era Kyivan Rus' state as their respective birthplaces, though this is the subject of much debate.[32]

Still, historian Timothy Snyder points to the Crimean War (1853–1856) as a turning point in the initial crystallization of the Ukrainian national identity and in Ukrainian perceptions of Russia and Russian perceptions of Ukrainians.[33] By this period, large swaths of modern-day Ukraine had been under Russian (and Polish) rule for over a century. However, the Tsarist regime's somewhat permissive approach to its culturally and ethnically

---

[30] Taras Kuzio, "Identity and Nation-Building in Ukraine, Defining the 'Other,'" *Ethnicities*, Vol. 1, No. 3, 2001, p. 344.

[31] Kuzio, 2001, p. 344.

[32] Kuzio, 2001, p. 347.

[33] Timothy Snyder, *The Reconstruction of Nations: Poland, Ukraine, Lithuania, Belarus, 1569–1999*, Yale University Press, July 2004, p. 121.

Ukrainian subjects prior to the 1820s meant that Ukrainians were freer to express their cultural identity while existing within the Tsarist system. The 1820s, however, ushered in a new period marked by greater repression at the hands of the tsarists and a growing movement of Ukrainian "folk patriotism from the West."[34]

Interestingly, these increased restraints on expressions of Ukrainian identity were tied to concurrent developments in Russian national identity. As Snyder notes, "[b]roadly conceived, Ukrainian culture was a bulwark of the Russian empire, providing many of its legitimating myths, its folksongs and folktales, and indeed its educated civil servants" in this period.[35] Thus, the consolidation of Russian national identity in this period, including via the adoption of the very narratives and cultural hallmarks Ukrainians were using to define their own sense of self, naturally pitted Ukrainian and Russian identities against one another. If certain traits were conceived of as inimitably Russian, they could not also be innately Ukrainian and vice versa. Rather, from Moscow's perspective, this meant that Ukrainians and Russians were indivisible, part of a single East Slavic, Russian nation.[36] We continue to see echoes of this tension today.

The realization in the latter half of the 19th century by the Tsarist regime that Ukrainians might seek to establish a separate identity and push for independence spurred policies designed to quash the continued development of a unique Ukrainian identity. Snyder cites the 1863 Valuev Decree, which proclaimed the Ukrainian language "has not, does not, and cannot exist," and the 1876 Ems Decree, which outlawed the production and importation of Ukrainian-language publications.[37]

These early disputes over cultural traditions and origin stories, magnified by Tsarist-era policies to extinguish the evolution of a Ukrainian national identity, emboldened the patriotic Ukrainian movements of the late 19th and early 20th century.[38] In turn, these developments only strength-

---

[34] Snyder, 2004, p. 121.

[35] Snyder, 2004, p. 121.

[36] Kuzio, 1998; Snyder, 2004, p. 122.

[37] Snyder, 2004, pp. 121–122.

[38] Kuzio, 1998, p. 3.

ened Russian resistance to the Ukrainian identity. Repressive Tsarist policies, such as language bans, forged the foundations for narratives of Ukrainian oppression at the hands of the Russian regime that have since become a core pillar of Ukrainian national identity.

Events in the 20th century only hardened these narratives. Although the Soviets relaxed linguistic and other restrictions on Ukrainians located in what is now the central and eastern part of the country in the 1920s (*Ukrainianization*) and promoted the inclusion of non-ethnic Russians in Soviet state positions (*korenizatsiia*), this period of relative freedom of expression was short-lived.[39] Soviet authorities quickly realized that by instituting permissive policies toward the Union of Soviet Socialist Republics (USSR)'s sizable ethnic minorities they had ceded authority and threatened their grip on power.[40] With that, Joseph Stalin not only reversed existing policies but also engineered new ones intended to marginalize and divide Ukrainians and prevent the development of their national identity. The purges of the 1930s hollowed out the Ukrainian intelligentsia, further stifling the consolidation of an activist Ukrainian community or identity.[41] Likewise, the Holodomor—a genocide of rural Ukrainians by way of a Soviet manufactured famine—killed millions of Ukrainians and left a lasting imprint on its survivors, one that persists as an important narrative for the Ukrainian national identity today.[42]

---

[39] As described by George Liber,

> In April 1923 the Russian Communist Party formalized the policy of *korenizatsiia* (indigenization or nativization) in order to defuse the hostility it provoked among the large non-Russian Soviet population during the Civil War. By promoting non-Russians into leading positions in the party, the government, and the trade unions and by subsidizing the development of distinct national cultures in the USSR, the party sought to legitimate a predominantly Russian and urban-based revolution in an overwhelmingly agricultural, multiethnic state. (George Liber, "*Korenizatsiia*: Restructuring Soviet Nationality Policy in the 1920s," *Ethnic and Racial Studies*, Vol. 14, No. 1, 1991, p. X. See also Kuzio, 1998, p. 5.)

[40] Kuzio, 1998, p. 5.

[41] George O. Liber, "Imagining Ukraine: Regional Differences and the Emergence of an Integrated State Identity, 1926–1994," *Nations and Nationalism*, Vol. 4, Issue 2, April 1999, p. 197.

[42] Liber, 1999, p. 192.

By the time that Ukraine declared its independence in 1991, Ukrainian narratives depicting Russia as the despotic other had been fused into the national identity for a majority of, although not all, Ukrainians. That said, the Russian regime was not the only external occupier having vied for control over Ukrainian lands or its peoples. In fact, in 1917, ethnic Ukrainians were divided between Austria-Hungary, Russia, and Romania.[43] But the post–World War II consolidation of Soviet rule over all Ukrainians; the painful, more recent experiences of the Soviet era; and Russia's continued aggressive behavior toward Ukraine in the post–Cold War period likely entrenched these views.

It is important to acknowledge, however, that this does not hold true for all Ukrainians at all points throughout the post–Cold War period. As we explain below, the Ukrainian identity is not homogenous. While we argue that the degree of contestation within Ukrainian national identity has diminished over the course of the post–Cold War period, particularly in the past decade, variation still exists. In certain pockets of Ukraine, views toward Russia, Russians, and Ukraine's relationship with Moscow have been positive. In this sense, Russia has not *exclusively* served as the other against which to define Ukrainian national identity (see section on contestation below for additional details).

Social Purposes—The Aims That Bind Ukrainians Together

Groups, including nations, are also bound by shared aims. Frequently, nations affix certain objectives to their collective sense of self, whether in the form of statehood or even the solidification of a unique national identity unto itself. The fundamental question associated with this feature is, "what common aims unify us."[44]

Though the aims central to Ukraine's contemporary national identity have evolved, several foundational goals have persisted. Perhaps the most prominent of these includes the establishment of a distinct Ukrainian identity and the establishment of an independent, sovereign state—one that is

---

[43] Kuzio, 1991, p. 2.

[44] Shulman, 1999, p. 1014.

free to choose its own political, economic, and social fate. This aim was most notably manifested in three areas: territorial integrity, energy independence, and Ukrainian language status, where the tensions between the post-Soviet and emerging Ukrainian identity of a newly independent nation were particularly consequential. This is not to say that all Ukrainians sought to cut all affiliation with Russia. Rather, they sought autonomy to make the decision to do so freely or not. As we explain above, this process has proved to be a struggle for several domestic and external reasons.

The Ukrainian and Russian authorities that ascended to power in the immediate aftermath of the USSR's collapse agreed on one core point—the Soviet system needed replacing.[45] However, Moscow and Kyiv held fundamentally different visions of what should replace it. Russia's first post-Soviet president Boris Yeltsin and other Russian authorities in the early 1990s wanted to preserve formal linkages among the former Soviet states in the form of a single economic market, a shared currency, a common military structure, and the centralized control of nuclear weapons.[46] Ukrainian authorities, by contrast, were opposed to the establishment of a new "supranational state controlled from Moscow," instead pushing for a fully autonomous state.[47] As scholar Paul D'Anieri notes, "even Kravchuk, who was elected Ukraine's president running *against* a nationalist, and had his highest support in eastern Ukraine and Crimea, adamantly refused to compromise Ukraine's sovereignty."[48]

Still, Ukraine's role as a Russian client state would prove difficult to disentangle. The overt and latent ties between Kyiv and Moscow endured long after Ukraine's declaration of independence. These have been pervasive, having penetrated nearly all facets of Ukraine's public and private spheres including the country's fledgling economy, political structures, media sector, military, and security services.[49] These early divergent perspectives

---

[45] D'Anieri, 2019, pp. 33–35.

[46] D'Anieri, 2019, pp. 34–35.

[47] D'Anieri, 2019, p. 35.

[48] D'Anieri, 2019, p. 35.

[49] D'Anieri, 2019, p. 32.

following the Soviet Union's collapse have fueled the antipathy plaguing Russian-Ukrainian relations since.

Chief among the linkages Russia has used to preserve control in Ukraine has been Ukrainian dependence on Russian energy, which persisted for decades following the collapse of the Soviet Union.[50] Many Ukrainian functionaries were convinced that Ukraine had no other option but to cooperate with Russia on energy, trying to negotiate favorable conditions for the purchase of the much-needed resources.[51] Others, though, viewed its dependence on Russia's energy as a threat to Ukraine's prospects as a sovereign state and explored ways to diversify its suppliers. During the repeated gas wars in the 2000s (see Chapter 2), Ukraine did not conform to Russia's efforts to sway its West-leaning government back toward more Kremlin-favorable policies.[52] Though Ukraine has ultimately made some concessions, its ability to withstand Russia's pressure at least for some time, was a vivid demonstration that Ukraine was not willing to trade democracy for gas.[53]

Moreover, Ukraine soon realized that the dependency was two-sided. As Gazprom's biggest customer at the time and a transit country, Ukraine has used this leverage to demonstrate to Russia that the gas wars could backfire. Likewise, Ukrainians became increasingly sensitive to Russia's manipulations, such as by offering cheaper natural gas in exchange for joining the Russia-led Eurasian Customs Union.[54] Unlike previous arrangements, this

---

[50] D'Anieri, 2019, p. 28.

[51] Oles M. Smolansky, "Ukraine's Quest for Independence: The Fuel Factor," *Europe-Asia Studies,* Vol. 47, No. 1, 1995.

[52] Richard B. Andres and Michael Kofman, "European Energy Security: Reducing Volatility of Ukraine-Russia Natural Gas Pricing Disputes," Institute for National Strategic Studies, National Defense University, *Strategic Forum,* No. 264, February 2011.

[53] Tetyana Yarmoshchuk, "Independent Ukraine 25: A Quarter Century of Gas Dependence?" ["Незалежній Україні 25: чверть століття газової залежності?"], Radio Svoboda, August 15, 2016; Alexander Motyl, "Ukraine vs. Russia: The Politics of an Energy Crisis," *Insight Turkey,* Vol. 7, No. 4, 2005.

[54] The Eurasian Customs Union was founded in 2000, and, as of 2022, consists of Russia, Belarus, Armenia, Kazakhstan, and Kyrgyzstan. See Kataryna Wolczuk, Rilka Dragneva, and Jon Wallace, "What Is the Eurasian Economic Union?" Chatham House, July 15, 2022; Mirror Weekly, "Russia Lures Ukraine into the Customs Union by Almost

one threatened to reverse the "civilizational choice" of Ukraine and was decisively rejected.[55]

The questions of Ukrainian national identity were pertinent not only on issues related to energy, or even foreign policy. In reality, with decision-making on reforms in practically any sphere (education, health care, social policy, defense), Ukraine was facing a choice of preserving the Soviet legacy or building a model that would, in the future, resemble its Western neighbors and partners. For Russia, Ukrainian democratization, accession to Western institutions, or dissolution of other ties have been viewed as threats.[56]

Ukrainian aims to establish an independent, democratic state have served as a powerful motivator driving Ukrainian society to choose what were often costly and painful reforms. Likewise, some Ukrainian authorities recognized that a strong democracy with the rule of law, free and fair elections, and effective domestic institutions that were also free of corruption was the best defense against an aggressive neighbor.[57] Membership in the EU, which gradually admitted former socialist nations around Ukraine, served as a beacon of these aspirations, and membership became one of the main national aims early in Ukraine's independence. In fact, the intent to integrate into the community of democratic European nations was expressed in "Main Directions of Ukraine's Foreign Policy," adopted by Ukraine's parliament in 1993 and further institutionalized in the partnership and cooperation agreement with the EU, signed by Leonid Kravchuk in

---

a Three-Fold Decrease in the Gas Price" ["Росія заманює Україну в Митний Союз майже триразовим зниженням ціни на газ"], October 9, 2012.

[55] Tetyana Sylina, "Allies or Fellow Prisoners?" ["У союзники чи у співв'язні?"], *Mirror Weekly*, April 8, 2011.

[56] Refer to Russia's actions toward Ukraine in the lead-up to the signing of the EU agreements in 2012–2013.

[57] Donii, 2020.

1994.[58] Though still in process, Ukraine obtaining EU candidate status in June 2022[59] was a significant milestone toward achieving this national aim.

Opinion polls show that the hardships that Ukraine endured (the membership application was submitted and candidate status granted after Russia's full-scale invasion in February 2022) only further strengthened the unity in understanding this goal as foundational for Ukraine's existence as a sovereign nation. In 2009, about 40 percent of Ukrainians supported EU accession.[60] In December 2021, 67.1 percent of respondents reacted positively to a question on whether they would vote in favor of EU membership on a referendum.[61] In October 2022, the membership was treated favorably by 86 percent of Ukrainians.[62]

A similar trend can be observed with another much more contested aim of Ukraine—NATO membership. Unlike EU accession, NATO membership was not declared an official foreign policy goal in the first years of Ukraine's independence. On the contrary, the Declaration of State Sovereignty of Ukraine "ceremoniously proclaim[ed] its intention to become a permanently neutral state in the future, which will be out of military [blocs]."[63] Understanding the fragility of newly formed nations and the inevitability of

---

[58] Parliament of Ukraine, "Main Directions of Ukraine's Foreign Policy" ["Про Основні напрями зовнішньої політики України"], 1993; European Union Law, Partnership and Cooperation Agreement Between the European Communities and Their Member States, and Ukraine, 1998.

[59] European Council and the Council of the European Union, "Ukraine," webpage, February 10, 2023.

[60] National Institute for Strategic Studies, "'Attitudes of Citizens Towards the Main Directions of Ukraine's Foreign Policy.' Analytical Memo" ["'Ставлення громадян до основних напрямів зовнішньої політики України.' Аналітична записка"], webpage, March 24, 2010.

[61] Kyiv International Institute of Sociology, "Attitudes Towards Ukraine's Accession to the EU and NATO, Attitudes Towards Direct Talks with Vladimir Putin and the Perception of the Military Threat from Russia: The Results of a Telephone Survey Conducted on December 13–16, 2021," press release, December 24, 2021.

[62] Ukrinform, "Ukraine Has a Record Level of Support for Joining NATO" ["В Україні - рекордний рівень підтримки вступу до НАТО"], webpage, October 3, 2022.

[63] Verkhovna Rada of the Ukrainian SSR, *Declaration of State Sovereignty of Ukraine*, 1990.

careful balancing between its neighbor and the West, Ukrainians hoped that neutrality could be the safest option. Even after the Orange Revolution of 2004, the support for NATO membership remained between 20 and 30 percent.[64] Politicians, including the pro-European ones, emphasized that this decision would never be adopted without getting popular support through a referendum. The latter is formally not required, but the pledges to hold one were important for acknowledging the different opinions on the country.

Nevertheless, Ukraine has deepened its cooperation with the Alliance throughout the post–Cold War period. The "Charter on a Distinctive Partnership between the North Atlantic Treaty Organization and Ukraine" was signed in 1997, and the first NATO-Ukraine summit was held.[65] Although the 2008 Bucharest summit did not result in opening a membership path, Ukraine continued to take part in a wide range of programs and initiatives, with NATO providing training to the Ukrainian military, strengthening its security system, and contributing to overall democratic development.[66] Recognizing that that accession was unrealistic, continued NATO cooperation gradually and informally turned into a goal unto itself.

Only as the hope for the normalization of Russia-Ukraine relations vanished after the annexation of Crimea did the support for NATO membership among the population start to increase. In 2015, some 40 percent of Ukrainians, based on various polling, said they would vote for NATO membership in a referendum.[67] In 2016, this number increased to almost 78 percent, with a rise of support in eastern Ukrainian regions.[68] The surveys conducted after the start of the full-scale invasion demonstrated that

---

[64] Olha Makarchuk, "Yushchenko—for a Referendum on EU and NATO Accession" ["Ющенко - за референдум відносно вступу до ЄС та НАТО"], BBC Ukrainian, undated.

[65] NATO, "Charter on a Distinctive Partnership Between the North Atlantic Treaty Organization and Ukraine," webpage, March 4, 2009.

[66] NATO, "Relations with Ukraine," webpage, February 22, 2023.

[67] Radio Svoboda, "Survey: 78% of Ukrainians Would Vote for Joining NATO in a Referendum" ["Опитування: за вступ до НАТО на референдумі проголосували б 78% українців"], July 6, 2016.

[68] Radio Svoboda, 2016.

NATO membership was treated favorably by a record-high number of Ukrainians—86 percent in October 2022.[69]

This increased support has translated into a more rapid movement toward further integration into NATO and, ultimately, desires for membership. In February 2018, President Poroshenko requested the Membership Action Plan for Ukraine as a formal step toward accession. In 2019, Ukraine's Constitution was amended to include NATO (and EU) membership as a national goal.[70] In September 2020, a new National Security Strategy for Ukraine was adopted, reiterating this aim as a national priority.[71] Two years later, amid the full-scale war, Ukraine formally applied for NATO membership.[72] While the process ahead remains unclear, crossing this line is undoubtedly significant.

Cognitive Models—How Ukrainians Interpret the World

Broadly speaking, cognitive models describe the unique lenses through which a group's members interpret the present and past and see the world. The core question here is, "how does who we are as a group shape how we see the world?" According to Brubaker, Loveman, and Stamatov, national

---

[69] Rating Group, "Foreign Policy Orientations of the Ukrainians in Dynamics (October 1–2, 2022)," webpage, October 3, 2022c.

[70] Parliament of Ukraine, "On Making Changes to the Constitution of Ukraine (Regarding the State's Strategic Course Towards Full Membership of Ukraine in the European Union and the North Atlantic Treaty Organization)" ["Про внесення змін до Конституції України (щодо стратегічного курсу держави на набуття повноправного членства України в Європейському Союзі та в Організації Північноатлантичного договору)"], 2019.

[71] President of Ukraine, "Decree of the President of Ukraine No. 392/2020: On the Decision of the National Security and Defense Council of Ukraine Dated September 14, 2020 'On the National Security Strategy of Ukraine'" ["Указ Президента України №392/2020: Про Рішення Ради Національної Безпеки і Оборони України від 14 вересня 2020 року «Про Стратегію національної безпеки України»"], September 14, 2020.

[72] Andrew E. Kramer, and Dan Bilefsky, "Ukraine Submits an Application to Join NATO, with Big Hurdles Ahead," *New York Times*, September 30, 2022.

identity is not just a "thing *in* the world, but a perspective *on* the world."[73] *Cognitive models* are "ways of recognizing, identifying, and classifying other people, of constructing sameness and difference, and of 'coding' and making sense of their actions. They are templates for representing and organizing social knowledge."[74]

One feature that commonly stands out in descriptions of Ukraine's national identity is *individualism*.[75] Throughout history, Ukrainians have been associated with a deep respect for individual freedom and dignity.[76] In Kyivan Rus', punishments for wrongdoings targeting one's honor, such as verbal or physical insults, were more profound than for inflicting material damage.[77] Corporal punishment was rarely used. In later periods of Ukraine's history, this respect for human dignity translated into the traditions of open communal institutions, or *hromadas*.[78] Members were free to leave or enter these institutions to pursue their own interests without repercussion.[79]

---

[73] Rogers Brubaker, Mara Loveman, and Peter Stamatov, "Ethnicity as Cognition," *Theory and Society,* Vol. 33, No. 1, February 2004, pp. 31–64.

[74] Brubaker, Loveman, and Stamatov, 2004, p. 47.

[75] Shulman, 1999, p. 1017.

[76] Shulman, 1999, p. 1017.

[77] Anton Oleinik, "On the Role of Historical Myths in Nation-State Building: The Case of Ukraine," *Nationalities Papers,* Vol. 47, No. 6, November 2019.

[78] The Ukrainian word *hromada* can be literally translated as *community*. Throughout history, Ukrainian peasants organized such communities that were ruled by local officials elected through democratic elections. The members of hromadas were free and able to make their own decisions regarding their farming needs and lives in general (V. A. Smoliy, ed., *History of Ukrainian Culture* [*Історія української культури*], Vol. 2, 2001, p. 848). This term has been also used to denote various organized resistance groups and societies in the Russian empire and later Soviet Union (Orest Subtelny, *Ukraine: A History,* 4th ed., University of Toronto Press, 2009). During the decentralization reform in the independent Ukraine that started in 2014, local communities were incentivized to amalgamate into self-governments called *Amalgamated Hromada* (AH) or, informally, hromada (Lucas Ford, "Understanding Ukraine's Decentralisation Reform," *Vox Ukraine,* June 22, 2020).

[79] Oleinik, 2019.

Historically, Ukraine's economy was also built on individualism. Individual farming remained a norm until Russian attempts to institute a communal system ultimately won out.[80] Russian communal institutions, on the contrary, exemplified collectivism where individual interests were subordinate to the collective.[81] Individualism is sometimes used to explain drastic differences in approaches to land use and responsibility for own welfare between Ukrainians and Russians, which are evident even from visual observations of Ukrainian and Russian settlements.[82]

While decades of living under Soviet rule left its mark on this facet of Ukrainian identity, the traditionally high value attributed to individualism and personal freedom has gradually returned since the collapse of the Soviet Union. The concept of individual freedoms and dignity were central to both revolutions in Ukraine in 2004 and 2014, with the latter aptly bearing the name "Revolution of Dignity." Public protests in both cases focused on the violation of Ukrainians' right to elect their leaders and to make geopolitical choices freely, without intrusion. Those who went to the streets or later joined the military did so to defend their freedom of choice, not in the name of a specific political cause.

In some parts of Ukraine, territorial pride was another important feature of Ukrainians' cognitive models, often over their national identity. Describing this phenomenon, some Western scholars use the term *tuteshni* (derived from the Ukrainian word *tut*, which can be translated as *here*).[83] While this particular word is very rarely, if ever, used in present-day Ukraine, the phenomenon of local patriotism has been heavily discussed in the national identity debates post-independence. On the one hand, it is acknowledged that throughout centuries of oppression, it was often the only way to openly express the feeling of belonging to Ukraine, love for Ukraine, and support for its freedom and independence.[84] On the other hand, it led

---

[80] Shulman, 1999, p. 1017.

[81] Oleinik, 2019, p. 1106.

[82] Reid, 2015.

[83] For instance, see Andrew Wilson, "Elements of a Theory of Ukrainian Ethno-National Identities," *Nations and Nationalism*, Vol. 8, No. 1, 2002; Reid, 2015.

[84] Donii, 2020, p. 298.

to distrust among people from different regions, especially from the capital. In the political domain, this phenomenon has translated into the preference for appointees with the same territorial origins.[85] Ukraine's president Leonid Kuchma was known for providing "favors," including in the form of appointments, to the representatives of his home region Dnipropetrovsk (currently Dnipro).[86]

This strong sense of belonging to local and regional communities is common for all of Ukraine's regions but has been particularly prevalent in the Donbas. This, however, did not translate into calls for the region's full independence or any form of reunification with Russia.[87] Political demands were rare and included political resignations, regional autonomy, and economic ties with Russia.[88] Russian identity in the east and south is much more tied to the Russian heritage and people, but not to the idea of unification with the state of Russia.[89]

That said, this trend of local and regional affiliation has diminished considerably since 2014, particularly since the invasion in 2022, in favor of a stronger sense of national self-identification. When asked "who do you consider yourself to be first of all" in November 2021 before the war, 20.8 percent of respondents chose "a resident of the village, district, or city in which [I] live." By December 2022, that figure had fallen to 7.9 percent nation-

---

[85] Donii, 2020, p. 179.

[86] Wilson, 2022, p. 194.

[87] Hrytsak, 1998.

[88] Al'ona Vyshnyts'ka and Anastasiya Vlasova, "A Strike. What Donbas Miners Remember About the Protests of the 90s" ["Страйк. Що пам'ятають шахтарі Донбасу про протести 90х"], *Hromadske*, August 24, 2019.

[89] John O'Loughlin, "The Regional Factor in Contemporary Ukrainian Politics: Scale, Place, Space, or Bogus Effect?" *Post-Soviet Geography and Economics*, Vol. 42, No. 1, January 2001.

wide.[90] Meanwhile, respondents selecting "a citizen of Ukraine" has grown steadily from 41 percent in 2000, to nearly 80 percent in December 2022.[91]

Individualism, respect for dignity, and territorial patriotism are reflected in another commonly mentioned trait of Ukraine's post–Cold War national identity; that is, strong support for democratic rule.[92] The origins of this mindset are often traced back to the political traditions of Kyivan Rus'.[93] Under this system, the monarch did not possess any "divine" authority.[94] Further, the prince's power was checked by the *viche*, a general assembly comprised of all citizens, regardless of social status.[95] As such, a strong (authoritarian) government is considered against Ukraine's tradition.[96] These features are often contrasted with Russians' practice of placing the ruler (czar) "only slightly below God."[97] Although the decisionmaking abilities of the viche were limited, it is believed to have given an impetus for later democratic developments such as the Coassak's establishment of general assemblies for decisionmaking.

Present-day Ukrainians have expressed similar sentiments. Opinion polls provide evidence of high support for democracy. For instance, the average score given to the importance of living in a democratic country

---

[90] "Sociological Monitoring 'Ukrainian Society' Public Opinion in Ukraine After 10 Months of War" ["Соціологічний моніторинг 'українське суспільство' громадська думка в Україні після 10 місяців війни"], *Kyiv Institute of Sociology of Ukraine*, 2023, p. 20.

[91] "Sociological Monitoring 'Ukrainian Society' Public Opinion in Ukraine After 10 Months of War" ["Соціологічний моніторинг 'українське суспільство' громадська думка в Україні після 10 місяців війни"], 2023, p. 21.

[92] Shulman, 1999.

[93] Shulman, 1999.

[94] Oleinik, 2019.

[95] Russia too has had similar institutions in its history, but the tendency toward highly centralized authority has prevailed in Russia's case over the centuries.

[96] City of Yours [Твоє місто], "'Language Is a Weapon, But Not the Main One.' Historian Yaroslav Hrytsak About How Russia Destroyed Ukrainian Language" ["'Мова— це зброя, але не головна.' Історик Ярослав Грицак про те, як Росія нищила українську"], webpage, undated.

[97] Shulman, 1999; Poe, 2000.

increased from 7.3 (out of 10) in 2011, to over 8 in 2017, and has remained fairly steady since.[98]

Ukrainian thinkers often contrast Ukrainian democratic tradition with Russia's history of highly centralized authority. Recent surveys have demonstrated that Russians are more willing than Ukrainians to sacrifice freedom and individual rights to preserve security.[99] The most recent waves of the World Values Survey also show some differences in attitudes toward the importance of democracy and freedom among Ukrainians and Russians. Ukrainians tend to be less confident in the government and political parties, scrutinizing their decisions and remaining ready to express discontent openly.[100] These trends might be an outgrowth of Ukrainians' historical memory, which cautions that one should expect betrayal (*zrada*) from any power holder.[101] While seemingly negative, this trait has likely served as leverage against authoritarian tendencies.

Lastly, Ukrainians have a longstanding tradition of using humor. Humor is believed to be an instrument for resistance to oppression and an effective mechanism to relieve tensions.[102] It was used in famous Ukrainian literary work by writers and poets in the Russian Empire and later the Soviet Union, helping to channel discontent with the political and social status of the Ukrainian nation and Ukrainians. With the start of Russia's full-scale invasion, Ukrainians leveraged laughter as a weapon of war. According to one estimate, even in the bloodiest first weeks of war, about 200 to 300 humor-

---

[98] Razumkov Centre, "Citizens' Assessment of the Situation in the Country, Trust in Social Institutions, Political and Ideological Orientations of Citizens of Ukraine Under Russian Aggression (September–October 2022)" ["Оцінка громадянами ситуації в країні, довіра до соціальних інститутів, політико-ідеологічні орієнтації громадян України в умовах російської агресії (вересень–жовтень 2022)"], webpage, October 28, 2022.

[99] Larysa Tamilina, "What Makes Us, Ukrainians, Different from Russians?" *Vox Ukraine*, March 24, 2022.

[100] Tamilina, 2022.

[101] Oleinik, 2019.

[102] W. S. Dubberley, "Humor as Resistance," *International Journal of Qualitative Studies in Education,* Vol. 1, No. 2, January 1, 1988; Owen H. Lynch, "Humorous Communication: Finding a Place for Humor in Communication Research," *Communication Theory*, Vol. 12, No. 4, 2002.

ous memes about the bravery of the Ukrainian military, attitudes toward Russian soldiers, and Western military aid were produced.[103] This form of accessible communication served Ukrainians well in that it put localized events into a broader cultural context, explaining many complex issues to audiences that were not familiar with them.[104]

Contestation—Homogeneity Within Ukrainian Identity

While groups are made up of individuals who not only share like traits, but agree on the characteristics that unite them, they still experience some degree of friction over members' conceptions of the group's identity. Put simply, contestation refers to the degree that a group's identity is debated by its members.[105] Some group identities are more disputed than others. What is more, the degree to which this is the case can evolve over time. This is the case with Ukrainian national identity.

Ukrainian independence in 1991 marked the first time that all Ukrainians were united within a single, autonomous, self-governed territory. Even so, the newly independent state inherited a fractured national identity. Writing in 1999, political scientist Stephen Shulman remarked that the "concentration of ethnic Russians and Russified Ukrainians in eastern Ukraine and the differing interpretations of the relationship of ethnic Ukrainian culture to Russian and European cultures hinder the extension of the nationalist vision of ethnic Ukrainian identity to the national level."[106] A survey he conducted in that same year led him to conclude that "while Ukrainian national integration is not in critical condition, it is beset by substantial problems."[107] Kuzio's research found the same. Several years later, Kuzio observed the

---

[103] Ukraine Crisis Media Center, "Humor as an Instrument of Resilience: How Ukrainians Laugh in Russia's Face?" webpage, December 11, 2022.

[104] Aja Romano, "Reckoning with the War Meme in Wartime," *Vox*, February 25, 2022.

[105] Abdelal et al., 2006, p. 700.

[106] Shulman, 1991, p. 1021.

[107] Shulman, 1999, p. 1026.

existence of two factions within the Ukrainian elite—one that favored ties with Europe and another with Russia.[108]

Decades after the declaration of Ukrainian independence and having undergone formative political events like the Orange Revolution (2004) and Revolution of Dignity (2013–2014), significant regional, linguistic, ethnic, and class differences affecting the identity-building process persisted.[109] In other words, contestation was high for much of the post–Cold War period. As we argue below, it was not until after Russia invaded in 2014 and its major assault in 2022, that the two faces of Ukraine's identity began to knit into a single whole.

Even though the overwhelming majority of Ukrainians voted in favor of independence in 1991, a study conducted by the Institute of Sociology of the National Academy of Sciences of Ukraine (NASU) in 2011, revealed that twenty years on, Ukraine remained divided on the question of independence along regional lines. According to NASU's polling, when asked in 2011, respondents in Kyiv, the West, the Center, and the North said they "would have voted in favor of independence by a considerable margin." Meanwhile, those in "the oblasts in the East and Crimea would have voted predominantly against independence, and in the South, public opinion was evenly divided."[110] Annual surveys revealed that a handful of factors—notably language distinctions, people's views on the legal and political status of the Russian language, and their preferences on Ukraine's alignment with Eastern or Western institutions—were the principal barriers dividing Ukraine throughout the post–Cold War period, including in 2011, when NASU conducted its study.[111]

The continued existence of the cleavages that Ukraine inherited can be, in part, attributed to their deliberate exacerbation by domestic and foreign political forces. Even though the 2004 Orange Revolution is seen as a for-

---

[108] Kuzio, 2001, p. 344.

[109] Iryna Bekeshkina, "Decisive 2014: Did It Divide or Unite Ukraine?" in Olexiy Haran and Maksym Yakovlev, eds., *Constructing a Political Nation: Changes in the Attitudes of Ukrainians During the War in the Donbas*, Stylos Publishing, 2017, p. 3.

[110] Bekeshkina, 2017, pp. 5–6.

[111] Bekeshkina, 2017, p. 6.

mative episode in Ukraine's post–Cold War political and cultural development, it also marked a period of internal disunity. The two leading candidates of the 2004 Ukrainian presidential elections, Kremlin sympathizer Viktor Yanukovych and his rival pro-Western Viktor Yushchenko, represented the two poles of Ukrainian national identity at the time. To marshal their respective constituencies within the electorate, each of the candidates played to Ukraine's internal divisions by promoting one of the two competing conceptions of Ukrainian identity, while denigrating the other. Yushchenko and his allies worked to "strengthen the ethnocultural foundation of national identity which manifested itself in more resolute promotion of the Ukrainian language and the nationalist narrative of Ukraine's history."[112] This, of course, marginalized Russophone populations comprising Ukraine's other half—a sentiment that Yanukovych and his Kremlin allies worked to agitate. Along with a platform that promoted a close association with Russia, Yanukovych also advocated for the rights of Ukraine's eastern and southern populations.[113]

In the years following the Orange Revolution, Ukrainian politicians continued to capitalize on these fissures.[114] As such, the Ukrainian public and its conceptions of identity remained largely divided along existing lines, surveys indicate. Attitudes toward the Euromaidan protests that erupted in late 2013—an event which is hailed as a significant step in Ukraine's development as a democratic state—reflect this polarization.[115]

In an important turn of events, evidence indicates that the Kremlin's aggressive behavior since 2014, intended to exploit the points of contestation within Ukrainian identity, produced the opposite effect. It motivated the consolidation of a more synergistic Ukrainian identity, more so than other domestic forces had before.[116] Available data reinforces these findings. As Figure 4.1 below illustrates, the events that transpired between summer 2013 and summer 2014—Russia's annexation of Crimea, invasion of the

---

[112] Kulyk, 2016a, p. 593.

[113] Bekeshkina, 2017, p. 6.

[114] Bureiko and Moga, 2019, p. 139.

[115] Bekeshkina, 2017, p. 8.

[116] Kulyk, 2016a.

FIGURE 4.1

Ukrainian Self-Identification as "Citizen of Ukraine"

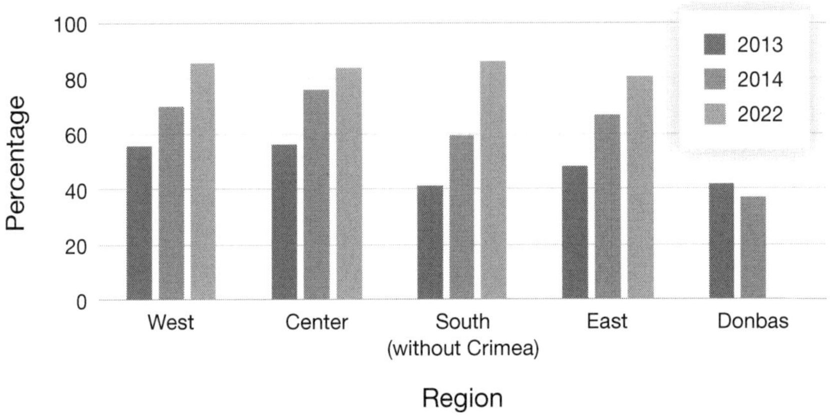

SOURCE: Figure features data presented in Bekeshkina, 2017, p. 14; and Kyiv International Institute of Sociology, "Indicators of National-Civic Ukrainian Identity," webpage, August 16, 2022. NOTE: The responses above were respondent replies to the question: "whom do you consider yourself first and foremost (2013–2014)?" In addition to the response above ("citizen of Ukraine"), respondents were also presented with the following options: "resident of the village, county, or city in which you live," "resident of the region (oblast or several oblasts) in which you live," "representative of your ethnos nation," "citizen of the former Soviet Union," "citizen of Europe," "citizen of the World," or "other."

Donbas, and the bloody events that have followed—appear to have had a profound impact on Ukrainians' sense of identity. In four of five regions polled (west, central, east, south) Ukrainians' self-identification as "citizens of Ukraine" increased by a relatively significant margin between June/ July of 2013 and July of 2014.[117] Here, the notable exception is the Donbas, where the proportion of respondents who cited their affiliation as citizens of Ukraine decreased slightly in this period.

Subsequent surveys revealed a slight slump in the level of expressed patriotism and national identification between 2014 and 2017. Nevertheless, the larger trend remains.[118]

---

[117] Bekeshkina, 2017, p. 14.

[118] Bekeshkina, 2017, p. 15.

One fundamental issue dividing Ukrainians for much of the post–Cold War period has been language. Ukrainian and Russian exist as two distinct, Slavic languages, both of which are used by Ukrainians today to varying degrees based on their region of origin, family history, and several other factors. While this issue is one that has plagued Ukrainian politics and society since independence in 1991, it is not a new issue. Rather, the language dispute in Ukraine has deep, complex roots.

Efforts to marginalize—and, in some periods, extinguish—the Ukrainian language while promoting the Russian language can be traced back centuries.[119] Tsarist authorities not only outlawed the publication of texts in the Ukrainian language but also forbade its use in schools, and in other official capacities.[120] As we explain above, in its embryonic years, the nascent Soviet government was forced to loosen restrictions on the Ukrainian language, instead adopting a policy of Ukrainianization.[121] This period was ultimately short-lived, however.

Beginning in the 1930s, Soviet authorities instituted policies designed to dilute Ukrainian national identity in favor of a Soviet (a Russo-centric) identity. As such, authorities relocated hundreds of thousands of ethnic Russians to what are now Ukrainian cities, a policy which planted the seeds for the urban-rural linguistic divide in Ukraine, whose vestiges remain visible today.[122] Following in Tsarist footsteps, Soviet authorities also enforced the use of Russian language instruction in primary and secondary schools and in public fora. Meanwhile most printed, visual, and audio media was produced in Russian.[123] Yet, despite Soviet attempts, the Ukrainian language remained a core pillar of Ukrainian nationalist identity throughout the Soviet period.

---

[119] Istorichna Pravda, "How They Fought with the Ukrainian Language. A Chronicle of Prohibitions for 400 Years" ["Як боролися з українською мовою. Хроніка заборон за 400 років"], webpage, July 3, 2012.

[120] George O. Liber, *Total Wars and the Making of Modern Ukraine, 1914–1954*, University of Toronto Press, 2016, p. 24.

[121] Kuzio, 1998, p. 5.

[122] Liber, 1999, p. 191.

[123] Liber, 1999, p. 192.

In fact, prior to the dissolution of the Soviet Union, Ukraine adopted a law, proclaiming Ukrainian the official language of the republic in 1989.[124] Despite attempts by Moscow to counter these initiatives, Ukraine continued its efforts and took a symbolic step of restoring the Ukrainian letter ґ (g) that was banned by Stalin in 1933,[125] later followed by a more consequential adoption of a state program for the development of Ukrainian language in February 1991.[126]

Even so, the question of Ukraine's official language became a highly polarizing and emotional issue for Ukrainian society, serving as a proxy for ethnic and political tensions in post-Soviet Ukraine.[127] In the first years following independence, Ukrainian nationalists advocated on behalf of the codification of Ukrainian as the sole language in official and social settings, whereas "Russian nationalists, communists, and many cosmopolitan liberals" campaigned for equivalent rights for both languages.[128] The latter group argued that a dual-language approach would protect the rights of Russophones. By contrast, those in favor of a singular national language (Ukrainian) felt that bestowing Russian with the equivalent legal status to Ukrainian would encourage its use as the *lingua franca*.[129] Others yet advocated for a middle path, with Ukrainian as the sole authoritative language

---

[124] Parliament of Ukraine, "On Amendments and Additions to the Constitution (Basic Law) of the Ukrainian SSR" ["Про зміни і доповнення Конституції (Основного Закону) Української РСР"], 1996; Kulyk, 2016b, p. 92.

[125] John-Thor Dahlburg, "It's Red-Letter Day for Ukraine as 'G' Makes Comeback: Linguistics: Banned by Stalin, the Letter Has Become a Symbol of the Struggle for Restoration of the Republic's Language," *Los Angeles Times*, November 30, 1991.

[126] Council of Ministers of the Ukrainian SSR, "About the State Program for the Development of the Ukrainian Language and Other National Languages in the Ukrainian SSR for the Period Until 2000" ["Про Державну програму розвитку української мови та інших національних мов в Українській РСР на період до 2000 року"], 1991.

[127] Dominique Arel, "Language, Status, and State Loyalty in Ukraine," *Harvard Ukrainian Studies*, Vol. 35, Nos. 1–4, 2017–2018; Dominique Arel, "Double-Talk: Why Ukrainians Fight Over Language," *Foreign Affairs*, March 18, 2014.

[128] Kulyk, 2016b, p. 92.

[129] Kulyk, 2016b, p. 92.

for symbolic reasons, while allowing Russian to prevail as the language of daily use for many Ukrainians.[130]

Before 2014, these divisions were deliberately perpetuated by political factions within Ukraine, with the aid of the Kremlin, which actively exploited the fractious language issues.[131] Yanukovych's Party of Regions passed a new law in 2012, which established Russian as a "regional" language. Likewise, Yanukovych's administration began rolling back educational requirements like that which mandated that high schoolers take university entrance exams in Ukrainian.[132] While the law changed little in practice for the millions of Russian-speaking Ukrainians in the country's southern and eastern regions, it was both celebrated and denounced by Ukrainians. On the one hand, those Ukrainians who viewed the Russian language as an expression of Soviet and Tsarist Russification policies condemned the move as a step backward toward the further dismantlement of Ukrainian identity.[133] On the other hand, Russian-speaking ethnic Ukrainians, who viewed post-independence Ukranianization policies as marginalizing, supported the law.[134]

These simmering issues came to a head again in 2014 with the Revolution of Dignity and the ousting of Yanukovych. On the heels of his departure, the new authorities in Kyiv called a vote to repeal the 2012 law.[135] "Although

---

[130] Kulyk, 2016b, p. 92.

[131] Yuliya Tyshchenko, "Language as a House of Existence" ["Мова як дім буття"], Ukrainian Independent Center for Political Studies, webpage, December 5, 2017.

[132] Tetyana Ogarkova, "The Truth Behind Ukraine's Language Policy," Atlantic Council, March 12, 2018; Parliament of Ukraine, "On Principles of the State Language Policy," 2012; Arel, 2014.

[133] Ogarkova, 2018; Ukrainian Week, "Events on July 5. Continuation of Protests for the Protection of the Ukrainian Language; the Debate Surrounding Lytvyn's Resignation; the First 52 Opposition Candidates for the Elections" ["Події 5 липня. Продовження протестів на захист української мови; дебати навколо відставки Литвина; перші 52 кандидати на вибори від опозиції"], webpage, July 6, 2012.

[134] Dominique Arel, "How Ukraine Has Become More Ukrainian," *Post-Soviet Affairs*, Vol. 34, Nos. 2–3, 2018, p. 187.

[135] Unian Information Agency, "The Verkhovna Rada Canceled Kolesnichenko's Language Law" ["ВР скасувала мовний закон Колесніченка"], webpage, February 23, 2014.

the move was blocked by the then acting president in order to prevent the use of allegations of discrimination against Russian to escalate the language conflict, it was nevertheless used by Russia as an excuse for the annexation of Crimea and the separatist fight in the Donbas."[136]

Importantly, evidence indicates that Russia's weaponization of the linguistic divide in this period pushed both Ukrainian factions to acknowledge the importance of unity over protective policies.[137] This trend was reflected in polling conducted by KIIS which indicated that the

> long-term numerical balance between supporters and opponents of the status of Russian as a state language on an equal footing with Ukrainian was broken, as a majority of Ukrainian citizens came to support the exclusive status of Ukrainian as the state language with provision for the local use of Russian.[138]

In fact, these events appear to have set the bearing for a longer-term trend in Ukrainian national identity.

Curiously, the results of nationwide surveys conducted by Rating Group indicate that, while the proportion of Ukrainians who self-identify as only speaking Ukrainian at home has remained relatively constant (between 43 and 51 percent) between November 2011 and March 2022, the proportion of those who say they spoke both Ukrainian and Russian has consistently grown from 15 to 32 percent in this period (Figure 4.2).[139] By the same token, the proportion of respondents who identified as Russian-only speakers at home has decreased from 40 percent in 2011 to 18 percent in 2022. Relatedly, when asked if/when they switched to the Ukrainian language, 31 percent of respondents in the south and 34 percent of respondents in the east said they began speaking Ukrainian more frequently as of August 2022.[140] These figures suggest that the segment of Ukrainians who spoke Russian exclusively before are now either learning the Ukrainian language or are choosing to

---

[136] Kulyk, 2016b.

[137] Kulyk, 2016b, p. 98.

[138] Kulyk, 2016b, p. 98.

[139] Rating Group, 2022a.

[140] Rating Group, 2022b, p. 38.

FIGURE 4.2

Self-Identification of Language Spoken "At Home"

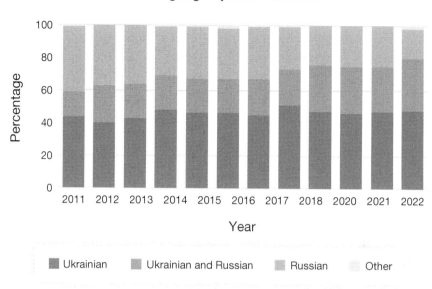

SOURCE: Figure features data collected and published by Rating Group, 2022a, p. 8.

incorporate it more in their daily lives. Thus, in a purely practical sense, the linguistic rift dividing Ukrainians throughout the post–Cold War period is narrowing.

While the figures above speak to the actual languages Ukrainians communicate in and might not necessarily reflect changes to Ukrainian perceptions on language policy, the results of another question in the Rating Group surveys suggests that the trend is being driven by patriotism and national identity rather than purely practical factors. Respondents were asked, "how should the Ukrainian and Russian languages coexist in Ukraine," a question which drives at Ukrainian attitudes on previously polarizing language policies.[141]

---

[141] Rating Group, 2022a, p. 11.

In April 2014, as Russian forces were infiltrating the Donbas, 47 percent of respondents selected "Ukrainian is the sole state language."[142] The remaining half of respondents were divided between "Ukrainian is the official state language, and Russian has official status in some regions" and "Russian language along with Ukrainian should have official status throughout Ukraine."[143] The survey's results show that the proportion of those supporting Ukraine as the sole state language has grown steadily year

FIGURE 4.3

Ukrainian Attitudes on Language Policy

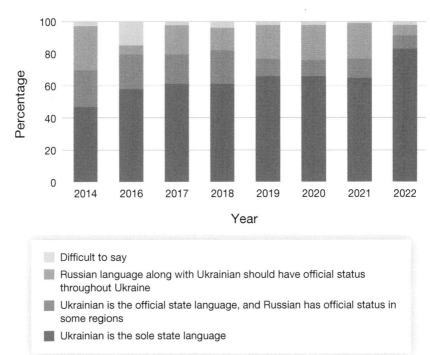

SOURCE: Figure features data collected and published by Rating Group, 2022a, p. 11.

---

[142] Rating Group, 2022a, p. 11.

[143] Rating Group, 2022a, p. 11.

over year. Meanwhile, the group of Ukrainians expressing support for Russian as a second state language have remained largely unchanged; that is, until Russia mounted its large-scale offensive in 2022.

The responses illustrated in Figure 4.3 point to an important shift in the level of contestation within Ukrainian national identity. Having just experienced Russia's large-scale invasion, the overwhelming majority (83 percent) of Ukrainians threw their support behind Ukrainian as the state's only official language when polled in March 2022. What is more, this trend largely holds across all of Ukraine's regions. Although fewer respondents in Ukraine's southern and eastern regions selected "Ukrainian is the sole state language" than did their counterparts in the central and western parts of the country, a solid majority still selected this option (63 and 76 percent respectively) in both regions.[144] This is to say that Russia's 2022 invasion has, the evidence would suggest, consolidated Ukrainian support around a more homogenous national identity nationwide.

Strength—Robustness of the Traits Binding Ukrainians

The last feature we will use to characterize Ukrainian national identity is *strength*. Shulman defines this feature as the "quantitative intensity of" the "feelings of solidarity among the peoples and regions of a state."[145] This factor is particularly challenging to examine because it requires us to assign a measure to the magnitude of Ukrainians' feelings and sense of identity, rather than describe its constituent elements. Fortunately, surveys offer insights on this issue too.

When asked what two emotions they felt when thinking about Ukraine in August 2022, the overwhelming first choice of Ukrainian respondents was "pride," which rose significantly from 34 percent a year earlier to 75 percent. The second most cited emotion was "sadness" at 29 percent, down 8 percent from a year earlier.[146] That said, stronger self-identification with feelings of patriotism among Ukrainians does not appear to be a new phenomenon. When asked "how would you describe yourself as a patriot of your coun-

---

[144] Rating Group, 2022a, p. 12.

[145] Shulman, 1999, p. 1015.

[146] Rating Group, 2022b, p. 38.

try, or not?" the overwhelming majority of respondents (at or above 75 percent) selected "yes, definitely" or "yes, relatively" between 2010 and 2020.[147] It stands to reason, given the direction of other related indicators like language and support for Ukraine's independence, that the strength of national identity is more robust than was the case prior to the war.

Conclusion

Now that we have characterized Ukrainian national identity, the question remains—how has its existence and evolution contributed to Russia's decision to invade its neighbor in the name of its own security and national interests? Our research sheds light on this question and the dynamics that begin to answer it.

First, the social purposes, or aims, that are foundational to Ukrainian national identity are fundamentally at odds with Russian conceptions of Ukraine's perceived regional role and its future. Though internally-focused, Ukrainians' domestic aims—political autonomy, economic independence, democracy, rule of law, free and fair elections, and the elimination of corruption—were nevertheless viewed as threats in Moscow. According to the Kremlin's zero-sum calculus, Ukrainian advancements toward democracy undermined Russia's longstanding role as the regional authority, particularly because such aspirations implied closer relations with the West—where these values and institutions are promoted—than with Russia—where they are not. In the foreign policy sphere, Ukrainian pursuits to gain accession into Western European economic institutions such as the EU were seen as jeopardizing Russian-led economic allegiances like the Eurasian Union. Yet, in the eyes of the Kremlin, Ukraine's cooperation with NATO has been the most contentious aim of all. President Putin explicitly expressed Russia's position on the issue during the 2007 Munich conference,[148] the 2008

---

[147] Rating Group, "About the Defender of Ukraine Day" ["До Дня захисника України"], October 2020, pp. 4–5.

[148] President of Russia, "Speech and the Following Discussion at the Munich Conference on Security Policy," press release, February 13, 2007.

NATO summit,[149] and numerous statements after that. Interestingly, as our analysis has shown, Russian attempts to inhibit Kyiv's pursuit of Ukrainian aims have backfired over time. The Kremlin's interference in domestic Ukrainian politics in 2004, and again in 2013–2014 to tip the scales in favor of Russian interests sparked considerable domestic responses in support of democratic progress and in protest to external meddling.

Likewise, the existence of a distinct Ukrainian national identity has fueled Russian aggression toward its neighbor. Evidence demonstrates that Russian leaders do not acknowledge the existence of a separate Ukrainian national identity. Recent Russian rhetoric—notably Putin's essay, "On the Historical Unity of Russians and Ukrainians"—has illustrated the Kremlin's position on this question. Writing in July 2021, Putin wholly rejected this notion, instead arguing that "Russians and Ukrainians [are] one people—a single whole."[150] Any debates over the so-called "national question" and attempts to "pit the parts of a single people against one another," said Putin, are manufactured by external forces. Putin does not appear to be alone in this view. According to surveys conducted by the Levada Center, an independent Russian polling outfit, at least half of Russian respondents selected "one nationality" when asked, "in your opinion, are Russians and Ukrainians one nationality or two different nationalities?"[151] These figures have waned since their peak in 2005, when 81 percent of respondents said Russians and Ukrainians are bound by a single, common nationality. Even so, 56 percent of respondents still expressed this view in March 2014, immediately following Russia's annexation of Crimea.[152]

Thus, efforts to preserve and develop Ukrainian national identity are viewed in Moscow as antagonistic to Russian conceptions of identity, which instead classifies Ukrainians as part of a broader eastern Slavic (and Russian) identity. In this respect, Belarus serves as an important foil to the Russian-Ukrainian relationship. Unlike the authorities in Kyiv and the

---

[149] Steven Erlanger, "Putin, at NATO Meeting, Curbs Combative Rhetoric," *New York Times*, April 5, 2008.

[150] President of Russia, 2021.

[151] Levada Center, "Russia–Ukraine Relations," press release, June 22, 2016.

[152] Levada Center, 2016.

Ukrainian public, "Belarusian President Alyaksandr Lukashenka largely accepts that Belarusians are a regional branch of Russians. Lukashenka does not therefore perceive Russia as a former 'imperialist' power."[153] This is a different perspective than that held by many Ukrainians throughout the post–Cold War period, including those Ukrainians who historically have sought closer economic ties with Russia, or those Russian-speaking Ukrainians who share some cultural traits with Russian counterparts. Research has shown that tendencies to lean toward Moscow rather than Brussels in some parts of Ukraine have largely been fueled by economic motivators, not an inherent self-identification with Russia.

What is more, the internal linguistic, regional, and political fissures that Ukraine inherited from the Soviet era have also served as a point of contention between Kyiv and Moscow. For much of the post-Soviet period, Russia has attempted to leverage these cleavages to weaken Ukrainian unity. It must be said, however, that they have not been alone in this approach; Ukrainian politicians have also exploited internal divisions in service of their own political gains. Paradoxically, however, our research suggests that Russia's decision to use force to achieve its aims in Ukraine has actually lessened internal contestation over Ukrainian national identity and has pushed Ukrainian identity to develop in ways that are less favorable to Kremlin ambitions. These include the broader use of Ukrainian language over Russian, greater support for accession to Western institutions, increasingly negative perceptions of Russia, and growing self-identification with a national Ukrainian identity, among others.

---

[153] Kuzio, 2001, p. 347.

CHAPTER 5

Conclusion

Russia's manipulation of Ukraine in the post-Soviet period and large-scale invasion in February 2022, was the result of the formation of a post-Soviet Russian identity that was hostile to the European project. That identity was the product of centuries of a Russian idea of an autocratic, Orthodox, and anti-Western great power. These characteristics are incompatible with Europe as it exists in the 21st century. The relative degree of unity in Europe on the political, economic, social, and security pillars of integration—and Russia's rejection of most of those pillars—reduces maneuverability in Russian alliance- and partnership-building in Europe and directs Russia to seek common cause with its closest neighbors on an alternative integration project that corresponds to Russia's self-image.

Contrary to Russian assertions, Ukraine's post-Soviet national identity was at odds with that of Russia. And the more Russia insisted that Ukraine was not what Ukrainians thought their country was, the more consolidated a distinct Ukrainian national identity took hold and the more stringent Ukrainian resistance to Russian manipulation became. One could argue that the most consequential promoter of the consolidation of Ukrainian national identity was Russia itself.

Various theories on manipulation, including those of the Russian special services, contend that successful outcomes begin with insight into the core beliefs and behavioral patterns of a target.[1] Armed with that information, an adroit manipulator can set conditions such that the object of manipulation will act in a way that seems perfectly aligned with self-interest but, in fact, is playing into the hands of the subject. Because of the closeness of the two

---

[1] Michael Weiss, *Aquarium Leaks: Inside the GRU's Psychological Warfare Program,* Free Russia Foundation, 2020.

countries in various aspects, Russia arguably should have been able to find a way to create conditions such that Ukraine would have willingly made decisions that corresponded to Russia's national identity and regional vision. But the 30-year confrontation between Russia and Ukraine that culminated with Russia's invasion demonstrated that there are limits to Russian manipulation. And the limits, in this case, stem from a Ukrainian national identity that Russia did not understand.

Abbreviations

CIS	Commonwealth of Independent States
CES	Common Economic Space
CSTO	Collective Security Treaty Organization
EEC	Eurasian Economic Community
EU	European Union
FSB	Federal Security Service
GUAM	Georgia, Ukraine, Armenia, and Moldova
NASU	National Academy of Sciences of Ukraine
NATO	North Atlantic Treaty Organization
NGO	nongovernmental organization
SBU	Security Service of Ukraine
USSR	Union of Soviet Socialist Republics

References

Abdelal, Rawi, Yoshiko M. Herrera, Alastair Iain Johnston, and Rose McDermott, "Identity As a Variable," *Perspectives on Politics*, Vol. 4, No. 4, December 2006.

Andres, Richard B., and Michael Kofman, "European Energy Security: Reducing Volatility of Ukraine-Russia Natural Gas Pricing Disputes," *Strategic Forum, National Defense University*, No. 264, February 2011.

Arbatov, Alexei G., "Russia's Foreign Policy Alternatives," *International Security*, Vol. 18, No. 2, Fall 1993.

Arel, Dominique, "Double-Talk: Why Ukrainians Fight Over Language," *Foreign Affairs*, March 18, 2014.

Arel, Dominique, "Language, Status, and State Loyalty in Ukraine," *Harvard Ukrainian Studies*, Vol. 35, Nos. 1–4, 2017–2018.

Arel, Dominique, "How Ukraine Has Become More Ukrainian," *Post-Soviet Affairs*, Vol. 34, Nos. 2–3, 2018.

Baranovsky, Vladimir, "Russia: A Part of Europe or Apart from Europe?" *International Affairs*, Vol. 76, No. 3, July 2000.

Bekeshkina, Iryna, "Decisive 2014: Did It Divide or Unite Ukraine?" in Olexiy Haran and Maksym Yakovlev, eds., *Constructing a Political Nation: Changes in the Attitudes of Ukrainians During the War in the Donbas*, Stylos Publishing, 2017.

Belin, Célia, James Goldgeier, Steven Pifer, and Angela Stent, "Russia's Ambitions, Ukraine's Resistance, and the West's Response," *Brookings*, March 28, 2022.

Berlin, Isaiah, *The Soviet Mind: Russian Culture Under Communism*, Brookings Institution Press, October 11, 2016.

Boudreaux, Richard, "Regional Outlook: Crimea's President a Prisoner of His Own Separatist Revolt: Russia has Lost Interest in Supporting Yuri Meshkov and His Would-Be Ministate," *Los Angeles Times*, May 23, 1995.

Brubaker, Rogers, Mara Loveman, and Peter Stamatov, "Ethnicity as Cognition," *Theory and Society*, Vol. 33, No. 1, February 2004.

Bruter, Michael, *Citizens of Europe? The Emergence of a Mass European Identity*, Palgrave Macmillan, 2005.

Burant, Stephen R., "Foreign Policy and National Identity: A Comparison of Ukraine and Belarus," *Europe-Asia Studies*, Vol. 47, No. 7, November 1995.

Bureiko, Nadiia, and Teodor Lucian Moga, "The Ukrainian-Russian Linguistic Dyad and Its Impact on National Identity in Ukraine," *Europe-Asia Studies*, Vol. 71, No. 1, February 2019.

Caro, Carlo J. V., "Vladimir Putin's 'Orthodoxy, Autocracy, and Nationality,'" Center for Ethics and the Rule of Law, University of Pennsylvania, August 31, 2022.

Charap, Samuel, and Timothy Colton, *Everyone Loses: The Ukraine Crisis and the Ruinous Contest for Post-Soviet Eurasia*, Routledge, 2017.

Charap, Samuel, Jeremy Shapiro, and Alyssa Demus, *Rethinking the Regional Order for Post-Soviet Europe and Eurasia*, RAND Corporation, PE-297-CC/SFDFA, 2018. As of July 16, 2023:
https://www.rand.org/pubs/perspectives/PE297.html

Chekh, Myroslav, and Ihor Hryniv, "The National Question: Ukraine as Europe" ["Національне питання: Україна як Європа"], *Mirror Weekly*, June 17, 2017.

City of Yours [Твоє місто], "'Language Is a Weapon, But Not the Main One.' Historian Yaroslav Hrytsak About How Russia Destroyed Ukrainian Language" ["'Мова—це зброя, але не головна.' Історик Ярослав Грицак про те, як Росія нищила українську"], webpage, undated. As of February 25, 2023:
https://tvoemisto.tv/exclusive/mova__tse_zbroya_ale_ne_golovna_istoryk_yaroslav_grytsak_pro_nyshchennya_ukrainskoi_movy_129710.html

Clement, Peter, "Analyzing Russia, Putin, and Ukraine at the CIA and Columbia," *Harriman*, Fall 2022.

Clunan, Anne L., *The Social Construction of Russia's Resurgence: Aspirations, Identity, and Security Interests*, Johns Hopkins University Press, 2009.

Cotton, James, "From Authoritarianism to Democracy in South Korea," *Political Studies*, Vol. 37, No. 2, 1989.

Council of Ministers of the Ukrainian SSR, "About the State Program for the Development of the Ukrainian Language and Other National Languages in the Ukrainian SSR for the Period Until 2000" ["Про Державну програму розвитку української мови та інших національних мов в Українській РСР на період до 2000 року"], 1991.

Dahlburg, John-Thor, "It's Red-Letter Day for Ukraine as 'G' Makes Comeback: Linguistics: Banned by Stalin, the Letter Has Become a Symbol of the Struggle for Restoration of the Republic's Language," *Los Angeles Times*, November 30, 1991.

D'Anieri, Paul, *Ukraine and Russia: From Civilized Divorce to Uncivil War*, Cambridge University Press, 2019.

Dawisha, Karen, *Putin's Kleptocracy: Who Owns Russia?* Simon & Schuster, 2015.

Dickinson, Peter, "How Ukraine's Orange Revolution Shaped Twenty-First Century Geopolitics," *Atlantic Council*, November 22, 2020.

Donii, Oles', *Transformation of the Ukrainian National Idea* [*Трансформація української національної ідеї*], Nash Format, 2020.

Dossani, Rafiq, Eugeniu Han, Cortez A. Cooper III, and Sale Lilly, *Democracy in the Asia-Pacific Region*, RAND Corporation, RR-A1515-1, 2021. As of June 29, 2023:
https://www.rand.org/pubs/research_reports/RRA1515-1.html

Dragneva, Rilka, and Kataryna Wolczuk, *Ukraine Between the EU and Russia: The Integration Challenge*, Palgrave Macmillan, 2015.

Dubberley, W. S., "Humor as Resistance," *International Journal of Qualitative Studies in Education,* Vol. 1, No. 2, January 1, 1988.

Erlanger, Steven, "Putin, at NATO Meeting, Curbs Combative Rhetoric," *New York Times*, April 5, 2008.

European Council and the Council of the European Union, "Ukraine," webpage, February 10, 2023. As of February 23, 2023:
https://www.consilium.europa.eu/en/policies/enlargement/ukraine/

European Union Law, Partnership and Cooperation Agreement Between the European Communities and Their Member States, and Ukraine, 1998.

Fisher, Max, "Putin's Case for War, Annotated," *New York Times*, February 24, 2022.

Fleron, Fredric J., Jr., "Post-Soviet Political Culture in Russia: An Assessment of Recent Empirical Investigations," *Europe-Asia Studies*, Vol. 48, No. 2, March 1996.

Ford, Lucas, "Understanding Ukraine's Decentralisation Reform," *Vox Ukraine*, June 22, 2020.

Foreign Affairs, "Was NATO Enlargement a Mistake?" April 19, 2022.

Fraser, Derek, "Taking Ukraine Seriously: Western and Russian Responses to the Orange Revolution," in Oliver Schmidtke and Serhy Yekelchyk, eds., *Europe's Last Frontier?* Palgrave Macmillan, 2008.

Freedom House, "Countries and Territories. Democracy Scores," webpage, undated. As of January 18, 2023:
https://freedomhouse.org/countries/freedom-world/scores

Fukuyama, Francis, *The Origins of Political Order: From Prehuman Times to the French Revolution*, Farrar, Straus, and Giroux, 2011.

Gaidar, Yegor, *Collapse of an Empire*, Brookings Institution Press, 2007.

Hajnal, J., "European Marriage Patterns in Perspective," in D. V. Glass and D. E. C. Eversley, eds., *Population in History: Essays in Historical Demography*, Edward Arnold LTD, 1965.

Henrich, Joseph, *The WEIRDest People in the World: How the West Became Psychologically Peculiar and Particularly Prosperous*, Farrar, Straus, and Giroux, 2020.

Hill, Fiona, and Clifford G. Gaddy, *Mr. Putin: Operative in the Kremlin*, Brookings Institution Press, 2015.

Holden, Gerard, *Russia After the Cold War: History and the Nation in Post-Soviet Security Politics*, Westview Press, 1994.

Hrytsak, Yaroslav, "National Identities in Post-Soviet Ukraine: The Case of Lviv and Donetsk," *Harvard Ukrainian Studies*, Vol. 22, 1998.

Hurak, Ihor, and Paul D'Anieri, "The Evolution of Russian Political Tactics in Ukraine," *Problems of Post-Communism*, Vol. 69, No. 2, 2022.

Ishiyama, John T., Michael K. Launer, Irina E. Likhachova, David Cratis Williams, and Marilyn J. Young, "Russian Electoral Politics and the Search for National Identity," *Argumentation and Advocacy*, Vol. 34, No. 2, 1997.

Istorichna Pravda, "How They Fought with the Ukrainian Language. A Chronicle of Prohibitions for 400 Years" ["Як боролися з українською мовою. Хроніка заборон за 400 років"], webpage, July 3, 2012. As of February 24, 2023:
https://www.istpravda.com.ua/digest/2012/07/3/89519/

Karaganov, Sergei, "Russia and the West After Kozyrev," Project Syndicate, September 2, 1995.

Kennan, George F., "A Fateful Error," *New York Times*, February 5, 1997.

Kiryukhin, Denys, "Roots and Features of Modern Ukrainian National Identity and Nationalism," *E-International Relations*, March 19, 2015.

Kokoshin, Andrei A., *Soviet Strategic Thought, 1917–91*, MIT Press, 1998.

Kozyrev, Andrei, *The Firebird: The Elusive Fate of Russian Democracy*, University of Pittsburgh Press, 2019.

Kramer, Andrew E., and Dan Bilefsky, "Ukraine Submits an Application to Join NATO, with Big Hurdles Ahead," *New York Times*, September 30, 2022.

Krickovic, Andrej, and Maxim Bratersky, "Benevolent Hegemon, Neighborhood Bully, or Regional Security Provider? Russia's Efforts to Promote Regional Integration After the 2013–2014 Ukraine Crisis," *Eurasian Geography and Economics*, Vol. 57, No. 2, 2016.

Kuchma, Leonid, *Ukraine Is Not Russia [Україна — не Росія]*, Vremia, 2004.

Kulyk, Volodymyr, "National Identity in Ukraine: Impact of Euromaidan and the War," *Europe-Asia Studies*, Vol. 68, No. 4, April 20, 2016a.

Kulyk, Volodymyr, "Language and Identity in Ukraine after Euromaidan," *Thesis Eleven,* Vol. 136, No. 1, October 1, 2016b.

Kuzio, Taras, "Ukraine: Coming to Terms with the Soviet Legacy," *Journal of Communist Studies and Transition Politics*, Vol. 14, No. 4, December 1998.

Kuzio, Taras, "Identity and Nation-Building in Ukraine, Defining the 'Other,'" *Ethnicities*, Vol. 1, No. 3, 2001.

Kuzio, Taras, "Nationalism, Identity and Civil Society in Ukraine: Understanding the Orange Revolution," *Communist and Post-Communist Studies*, Vol. 43, No. 3, September 1, 2010.

Kyiv International Institute of Sociology, "Attitudes Towards Ukraine's Accession to the EU and NATO, Attitudes Towards Direct Talks with Vladimir Putin and the Perception of the Military Threat from Russia: The Results of a Telephone Survey Conducted on December 13–16, 2021," press release, December 24, 2021.

Kyiv International Institute of Sociology, "Indicators of National-Civic Ukrainian Identity," webpage, August 16, 2022. As of July 18, 2023: https://www.kiis.com.ua/?lang=eng&cat=reports&id=1131&page=1

Lambroschini, Sophie, "Russia/Ukraine: Prime Ministers Meet Today over Tuzla Dam Dispute," *Radio Free Europe/Radio Liberty*, October 24, 2003.

Larrabee, Stephen F., "Russia, Ukraine, and Central Europe: The Return of Geopolitics," *Journal of International Affairs,* Vol. 63, No. 2, 2010.

Laruelle, Marlène, *Russian Eurasianism: Ideology of Empire*, Johns Hopkins University Press, 2012.

Levada Center, "Press-vypusk No. 32: 13 noiabria 2001 goda," November 13, 2001.

Levada Center, "Russia–Ukraine Relations," press release, June 22, 2016.

Liber, George, "Korenizatsiia: Restructuring Soviet Nationality Policy in the 1920s," *Ethnic and Racial Studies*, Vol. 14, No. 1, 1991.

Liber, George O., "Imagining Ukraine: Regional Differences and the Emergence of an Integrated State Identity, 1926–1994," *Nations and Nationalism*, Vol. 4, Issue 2, April 1999.

Liber, George O., *Total Wars and the Making of Modern Ukraine, 1914–1954*, University of Toronto Press, 2016.

Lieven, Anatol, *Ukraine and Russia: A Fraternal Rivalry*, United States Institute of Peace, 1999.

Lutsevych, Orysia, and Jon Wallace, "Ukraine-Russia Relations," Chatham House, March 24, 2022.

Lynch, Owen H., "Humorous Communication: Finding a Place for Humor in Communication Research," *Communication Theory*, Vol. 12, No. 4, 2002.

Makarchuk, Olha, "Yushchenko—for a Referendum on EU and NATO Accession" ["Ющенко - за референдум відносно вступу до ЄС та НАТО"], BBC Ukrainian, undated.

Malcolm, Neil, and Alex Pravda, "Democratization and Russian Foreign Policy," *International Affairs*, Vol. 72, No. 3, July 1996.

McFaul, Michael, "Russia's Road to Autocracy," *Journal of Democracy*, Vol. 32, No. 4, October 2021.

Mezentsev, Yaroslav, "Cold War for Crimea. How the Fleet Was Divided in the 1990s," *Istoreechna Pravda*, May 10, 2011.

Miller, Greg, and Catherine Belton, "Russia's Spies Misread Ukraine and Misled Kremlin as War Loomed," *Washington Post*, August 19, 2022.

Mirror Weekly, "Russia Lures Ukraine Into the Customs Union by Almost a Three-Fold Decrease in the Gas Price" ["Росія заманює Україну в Митний Союз майже триразовим зниженням ціни на газ"], October 9, 2012.

Mitterauer, Michael, and Alexander Kagan, "Russian and Central European Family Structures: A Comparative View," *Journal of Family History*, Spring 1982.

Mokyr, Joel, *A Culture of Growth: The Origins of the Modern Economy*, Princeton University Press, 2010.

Motyl, Alexander J., "Ukraine vs. Russia: The Politics of an Energy Crisis," *Insight Turkey*, Vol. 7, No. 4, 2005.

Motyl, Alexander J., "The Language of Russia's War on Ukraine," *Foreign Policy*, March 13, 2022.

Murphy, Kim, "Russia-Ukraine Ties Founder on the Shore of Tiny Isle," *Los Angeles Times*, November 3, 2003.

National Institute for Strategic Studies, "'Attitudes of Citizens Towards the Main Directions of Ukraine's Foreign Policy.' Analytical Memo" ["Ставлення громадян до основних напрямів зовнішньої політики України." Аналітична записка"], webpage, March 24, 2010. As of February 24, 2023: http://niss.gov.ua/doslidzhennya/mizhnarodni-vidnosini/ stavlennya-gromadyan-do-osnovnikh-napryamiv-zovnishnoi-politiki

NATO—*See* North Atlantic Treaty Organization.

Nicholaides, Nicholas, "Russia Needs Novorossiya," Geopolitica.ru, October 18, 2017.

North Atlantic Treaty Organization, "Charter on a Distinctive Partnership between the North Atlantic Treaty Organization and Ukraine," webpage, March 4, 2009. As of February 24, 2023:
https://www.nato.int/cps/en/natohq/official_texts_25457.htm

North Atlantic Treaty Organization, "Relations with Ukraine," webpage, February 22, 2023. As of February 24, 2023:
https://www.nato.int/cps/en/natohq/topics_37750.htm

Obshchestvennoe mnenie-2014, Levada-Tsentr, Moscow, 2014, p. 28.

O'Loughlin, John, "The Regional Factor in Contemporary Ukrainian Politics: Scale, Place, Space, or Bogus Effect?" *Post-Soviet Geography and Economics,* Vol. 42, No. 1, January 2001.

Ogarkova, Tetyana, "The Truth Behind Ukraine's Language Policy," Atlantic Council, March 12, 2018.

Oleinik, Anton, "On the Role of Historical Myths in Nation-State Building: The Case of Ukraine," *Nationalities Papers,* Vol. 47, No. 6, November 2019.

"Opposition to NATO Expansion," Arms Control Association, June 26, 1997.

Parliament of Ukraine, "Main Directions of Ukraine's Foreign Policy" ["Про Основні напрями зовнішньої політики України"], 1993. As of February 23, 2023:
https://zakon.rada.gov.ua/go/3360-12

Parliament of Ukraine, "On Amendments and Additions to the Constitution (Basic Law) of the Ukrainian SSR" ["Про зміни і доповнення Конституції (Основного Закону) Української РСР"], 1996. As of February 24, 2023:
https://zakon.rada.gov.ua/go/8303-11

Parliament of Ukraine, "On Principles of the State Language Policy" "[Про засади державної мовної політики]," 2012. As of February 24, 2023:
https://zakon.rada.gov.ua/go/5029-17

Parliament of Ukraine, "On Making Changes to the Constitution of Ukraine (Regarding the State's Strategic Course Towards Full Membership Of Ukraine in the European Union and the North Atlantic Treaty Organization)" ["Про внесення змін до Конституції України (щодо стратегічного курсу держави на набуття повноправного членства України в Європейському Союзі та в Організації Північноатлантичного договору)"], 2019. As of February 24, 2023:
https://zakon.rada.gov.ua/go/2680-19

Paul, Christopher, Michael Schwille, Michael Vasseur, Elizabeth M. Bartels, and Ryan Bauer, *The Role of Information in U.S. Concepts for Strategic Competition,* RAND Corporation, RR-A1256-1, 2022. As of July 14, 2023:
https://www.rand.org/pubs/research_reports/RRA1256-1.html

Pipes, Richard, *Russia Under the Old Regime*, Penguin Books, 2nd ed., 1997.

Pipes, Richard, *Russian Conservatism and Its Critics: A Study in Political Culture*, Yale University Press, 2007.

Plokhy, Serhii, "The Ghosts of Pereyaslav: Russo-Ukrainian Historical Debates in the Post-Soviet Era," *Europe-Asia Studies*, Vol. 53, No. 3, 2001.

Plokhy, Serhii, *Lost Kingdom: The Quest for Empire and the Making of the Russian Nation*, Basic Books, 2017.

Poe, Marshall T., *"A People Born to Slavery": Russia in Early Modern European Ethnography, 1476–1748*, Cornell University Press, 2000.

President of Russia, "Speech and the Following Discussion at the Munich Conference on Security Policy," press release, February 13, 2007.

President of Russia, "Address by President of Russian Federation," press release, March 18, 2014.

President of Russia, "On the Historical Unity of Russians and Ukrainians," press release, July 12, 2021.

President of Russia, "Address by the President of the Russian Federation," press release, February 21, 2022.

President of Ukraine, "Decree of the President of Ukraine No. 392/2020: On the Decision of the National Security and Defense Council of Ukraine Dated September 14, 2020 'On the National Security Strategy of Ukraine'" ["Указ Президента України №392/2020: Про Рішення Ради Національної Безпеки і Оборони України від 14 вересня 2020 року «Про Стратегію національної безпеки України»"], September 14, 2020. As of February 24, 2023:
https://www.president.gov.ua/documents/3922020-35037

Putin, Vladimir, "Annual Address to the Federal Assembly of the Russian Federaton," speech, May 26, 2004.

Radio Svoboda, "Survey: 78% of Ukrainians Would Vote for Joining NATO in a Referendum" ["Опитування: за вступ до НАТО на референдумі проголосували б 78% українців"], July 6, 2016.

Rating Group, "About the Defender of Ukraine Day" ["До Дня захисника України"], October 2020.

Rating Group, "The Sixth National Poll: The Language Issue in Ukraine (March 19, 2022)," webpage, March 25, 2022a. As of February 24, 2023:
https://ratinggroup.ua/en/research/ukraine/language_issue_in_ukraine_march_19th_2022.html

Rating Group, "Seventeenth National Survey: Identity. Patriotism. Values (August 17–18, 2022)," webpage, August 17, 2022b. As of February 21, 2023:
http://ratinggroup.ua/en/research/ukraine/s_mnadcyate_zagalnonac_onalne_opituvannya_dentichn _st_patr_otizm_c_nnost_17-18_serpnya_2022.html

Rating Group, "Foreign Policy Orientations of the Ukrainians in Dynamics (October 1–2, 2022)," webpage, October 3, 2022c. As of February 25, 2023: http://ratinggroup.ua/en/research/ukraine/dinam_ka_zovn_shno-pol_tichnih_nastro_v_naselennya_1-2_zhovtnya_2022.html

Razumkov Centre, "Citizens' Assessment of the Situation in the Country, Trust in Social Institutions, Political and Ideological Orientations of Citizens of Ukraine Under Russian Aggression (September–October 2022)" ["Оцінка громадянами ситуації в країні, довіра до соціальних інститутів, політико-ідеологічні орієнтації громадян України в умовах російської агресії (вересень–жовтень 2022)"], webpage, October 28, 2022. As of February 25, 2023: https://razumkov.org.ua/napriamky/sotsiologichni-doslidzhennia/otsinka-gromadianamy-sytuatsii-v-kraini-dovira-do-sotsialnykh-instytutiv-politykoideologichni-oriientatsii-gromadian-ukrainy-v-umovakh-rosiiskoi-agresii-veresen-zhovten-2022r

Reach, Clint, "China and Russia in Contemporary Ideological Competition," 2020.

Reach, Clint, "The Origins of Russian Conduct," *PRISM*, Vol. 9, No. 3, November 2021.

Reid, Anna, *Borderland: A Journey Through the History of Ukraine*, Basic Books, 2015.

Romano, Aja, "Reckoning with the War Meme in Wartime," *Vox*, February 25, 2022.

Roslycky, Lada L., "Russia's Smart Power in Crimea: Sowing the Seeds of Trust," *Southeast European and Black Sea Studies*, Vol. 11, No. 3, September 2011.

Sharafutdinova, Gulnaz, *The Red Mirror: Putin's Leadership and Russia's Insecure Identity*, Oxford University Press, October 2020.

Shevtsova, Lilia, *Lonely Power: Why Russia Has Failed to Become the West and the West is Weary of Russia*, Carnegie Endowment for International Peace, 2010, p. 160.

Shogren, Elizabeth, "In the Shadow of 'Big Brother': Ukraine: Long Under Russia's Thumb, the Newly Independent State Struggles to Change Its Relationship to One of Equals," *Los Angeles Times*, May 1, 1992.

Shulman, Stephen, "The Cultural Foundations of Ukrainian National Identity," Ethnic and Racial Studies, Vol. 22, No. 6, November 1999.

Shulman, Stephen, "The Contours of Civic and Ethnic National Identification in Ukraine," *Europe-Asia Studies*, Vol. 56, No. 1, January 1, 2004.

Smolansky, Oles M., "Ukraine's Quest for Independence: The Fuel Factor," *Europe-Asia Studies*, Vol. 47, No. 1, 1995.

Smoliy, V. A., ed., *History of Ukrainian Culture [Історія української культури]*, Vol. 2, 2001.

Snyder, Timothy, *The Reconstruction of Nations: Poland, Ukraine, Lithuania, Belarus, 1569–1999*, Yale University Press, July 2004.

"Sociological Monitoring 'Ukrainian Society' Public Opinion in Ukraine After 10 Months of War" ["Соціологічний моніторинг 'українське суспільство' громадська думка в Україні після 10 місяців війни"], *Institute of Sociology of Ukraine*, 2023.

Socor, Vladimir, "Azov Sea, Kerch Strait: Evolution of Their Purported Legal Status (Part Two)," *Jamestown Foundation*, December 5, 2018.

Solzhenitsyn, Aleksandr, *Rebuilding Russia: Reflections and Tentative Proposals*, Harper Collins Publishers, 1991.

Stebelsky, Ihor, "Ethnic Self-Identification in Ukraine, 1989–2001: Why More Ukrainians and Fewer Russians?" *Canadian Slavonic Papers*, Vol. 51. No, 1, March 2009.

Stern, Jonathan, Simon Pirani, and Katja Yafimava, "The Russo-Ukrainian Gas Dispute of January 2009: A Comprehensive Assessment," Oxford Institute for Energy Studies, February 2009.

Subtelny, Orest, *Ukraine: A History*, 4th ed., University of Toronto Press, 2009.

Svarin, David, "The Construction of 'Geopolitical Spaces' in Russian Foreign Policy Discourse Before and After the Ukraine Crisis," *Journal of Eurasian Studies*, No. 7, 2016.

Sylina, Tetyana, "Allies or Fellow Prisoners?" ["У союзники чи у співв'язні?"], *Mirror Weekly*, April 8, 2011.

Tamilina, Larysa, "What Makes Us, Ukrainians, Different from Russians?" *Vox Ukraine*, March 24, 2022.

Taylor, Brian, *The Code of Putinism*, Oxford University Press, 2018.

Tharoor, Ishaan, "How Russia's Invasion Strengthened Ukrainian Identity," *Washington Post*, August 24, 2022.

Thelen, Shawn T., and Earl D. Honeycutt, Jr., "National Identity in Russia Between Generations Using the National Identity Scale," *Journal of International Marketing*, Vol. 12, No. 2, 2004.

Tolz, Vera, "Forging the Nation: National Identity and Nation Building in Post-Communist Russia," *Europe-Asia Studies*, Vol. 50, No. 6, September 1998.

Trenin, Dmitry, "The End of Eurasia: Russia on the Border Between Geopolitics and Globalization," Carnegie Endowment for International Peace, 2002.

Trenin, Dmitry, "Russia's Breakout from the 'Post-Cold War System,'" Carnegie Moscow Center, 2013.

Tsygankov, Andrei P., *The Strong State in Russia: Development and Crisis*, Oxford University Press, 2015.

Tyshchenko, Yuliya, "Language as a House of Existence" ["Мова як дім буття"], Ukrainian Independent Center for Political Studies, webpage, December 5, 2017. As of February 24, 2023:
http://www.ucipr.org.ua/ua/kontakti/statt/mova-yak-d-m-buttya

Ukraine Crisis Media Center, "Humor as an Instrument of Resilience: How Ukrainians Laugh in Russia's Face?" webpage, December 11, 2022. As of February 24, 2023:
https://uacrisis.org/en/ukraine-in-flames-276

Ukrainian Week, "Events on July 5. Continuation of Protests for the Protection of the Ukrainian Language; the Debate Surrounding Lytvyn's Resignation; the First 52 Opposition Candidates for the Elections" ["Події 5 липня. Продовження протестів на захист української мови; дебати навколо відставки Литвина; перші 52 кандидати на вибори від опозиції"], webpage, July 6, 2012. As of February 24, 2023:
https://tyzhden.ua/podii-5-lypnia-prodovzhennia-protestiv-na-zakhyst-ukrainskoi-movy-debaty-navkolo-vidstavky-lytvyna-pershi-52-kandydaty-na-vybory-vid-opozytsii/

"Ukrainian Woman Offers Seeds to Russian Soldiers So 'Sunflowers Grow When They Die'," *The Guardian*, February 25, 2022.

Ukrinform, "Ukraine has a Record Level of Support for Joining NATO" ["В Україні - рекордний рівень підтримки вступу до НАТО"], webpage, October 3, 2022. As of February 24, 2023:
https://www.ukrinform.ua/rubric-polytics/3584786-v-ukraini-rekordnij-riven-pidtrimki-vstupu-do-nato.html

Unian Information Agency, "The Verkhovna Rada Canceled Kolesnichenko's Language Law" ["ВР скасувала мовний закон Колесніченка"], webpage, February 23, 2014. As of February 24, 2023:
https://www.unian.ua/politics/888625-vr-skasuvala-movniy-zakon-kolesnichenka.html

Urban, Michael, "Contending Conceptions of Nation and State in Russian Politics: Defining Ideologies in Post-Soviet Russia," *Demokratizatsiya*, Vol. 1, No. 4, 1992.

Urban, Michael, "The Politics of Identity in Russia's Postcommunist Transition: The Nation Against Itself," *Slavic Review*, Vol. 53, No. 3, Autumn 1994.

Varettoni, William, "Crimea's Overlooked Instability," *Washington Quarterly*, Vol. 34, No. 3, 2011.

Verkhovna Rada of the Ukrainian SSR, *Declaration of State Sovereignty of Ukraine*, 1990. As of March 5, 2023:
https://zakon.rada.gov.ua/go/55-12

Vyshnyts'ka, Al'ona, and Anastasiya Vlasova, "A Strike. What Donbas Miners Remember About the Protests of the 90s" ["Страйк. Що пам'ятають шахтарі Донбасу про протести 90х"], *Hromadske*, August 24, 2019.

Watts, Stephen, Nathan Beauchamp-Mustafaga, Benjamin N. Harris, and Clint Reach, "Alternative Worldviews: Appendixes," RAND Corporation, RR-2982, 2020. As of October 2, 2023:
https://www.rand.org/content/dam/rand/pubs/research_reports/RR2900/RR2982/RAND_RR2982.appendixes.pdf

Weiss, Michael, *Aquarium Leaks: Inside the GRU's Psychological Warfare Program*, Free Russia Foundation, 2020.

Wilson, Andrew, "Elements of a Theory of Ukrainian Ethno-National Identities," *Nations and Nationalism*, Vol. 8, No. 1, 2002.

Wilson, Andrew, *The Ukrainians: Unexpected Nation*, 5th ed., Yale University Press, 2022.

Wolczuk, Kataryna, Rilka Dragneva, and Jon Wallace, "What Is the Eurasian Economic Union?" Chatham House, July 15, 2022.

Yarmoshchuk, Tetyana, "Independent Ukraine 25: A Quarter Century of Gas Dependence?" ["Незалежній Україні 25: чверть століття газової залежності?"], Radio Svoboda, August 15, 2016.

"Yeltsin Assails Parliament Vote Claiming Crimean Port for Russia," r*New York Times*, July 11, 1993.

Young, Thomas, "10 Maps That Explain Ukraine's Struggle for Independence," *Brookings*, May 21, 2015.

Ziblatt, Daniel, "How Did Europe Democratize," *World Politics*, Vol. 58, No. 2, January 2006.

Zimmerman, William, "Is Ukraine a Political Community?" *Communist and Post-Communist Studies*, Vol. 31, No. 1, 1998.